D1297888

Documenting Maritime Folklife
An Introductory Guide

By David A. Taylor

Library of Congress   Washington 1992

Publications of the American Folklife Center, No. 18

Documenting Maritime Folklife is a product of a joint project of the American Folklife Center and the Bureau of Florida Folklife Programs, Florida Department of State.

Cover: Waterman Alex Kellam of Crisfield, Maryland, (left) with his friend Charlton Marshall and their catch of rockfish. Photo in Kellam's album copied by Carl Fleischhauer (AFC 45/28).

Library of Congress Cataloging-in-Publication Data

Taylor, David Alan, 1951–
        Documenting maritime folklife: an introductory guide/by David
A. Taylor.
              p. cm.—(Publications of the American Folklife Center; no.
18)
        Includes bibliographical references.
        ISBN 0–8444–0721–6
—— —— Copy 3 Z663. 116 .D63 1992
        1. Folklore—Methodology. 2. Maritime anthropology. 3. Maritime
anthropology—United States. 4. Seafaring life—Folklore.
5. Seafaring life—United States—Folklore. I. Title. II Series.
GR40.T39 1992
398' .01–dc20   91–36699
                                                                CIP

For sale by the U.S. Government Printing Office
Superintendent of Documents, Mail Stop: SSOP, Washington, DC 20402-9328

Contents

Preface

Documenting Maritime Folklife has two main purposes: to promote understanding of maritime cultural heritage (the body of locally distinctive traditional knowledge found wherever groups of people live near oceans, rivers, lakes, and streams); and to provide an introduction to the methods for identifying and documenting common maritime traditions. The guide is intended for nonprofessional researchers and community groups who wish to explore their own maritime cultural heritage. But it may also be useful to professionals in fields such as marine biology, fisheries extension, community planning, and education who are trying to understand the cultural aspects of maritime activities, as well as to students and lay persons working on projects under the direction of professional folklorists, anthropologists, historians, preservationists, cultural geographers, and other specialists in cultural studies.

In addition to examples of common maritime traditions and the methods that can be used to document them, *Documenting Maritime Folklife* includes suggestions for projects to disseminate collected information and appendixes containing examples of fieldnotes, a step-by-step description of the documentation of a small boat's hull

Painting of shrimp boat and its crew on the side of a seafood processing building in Apalachicola, Florida. Photo by David A. Taylor (FMP86–BDT029/2)

shape, and sample forms for collecting and organizing information and obtaining informants' consent. A bibliography of important publications supplements the resources provided here.

Documenting Maritime Folklife seeks to open the door to maritime culture and its documentation. It does not pretend to be a comprehensive survey of all the manifestations or all the theories and documentation methods cultural investigators have used to record and analyze them. Neither does it offer a thorough discussion of contemporary issues pertaining to maritime culture. Readers who wish to explore the subject further should consult the bibliography.

Work on *Documenting Maritime Folklife* began in July 1986, when I tested documentation techniques in the fishing village of Mayport, on the northeast coast of Florida. Following two months of fieldwork in Mayport, I wrote a first draft for the guide, which was then tested by a team of folklorists from the Bureau of Florida Folklife Programs and an anthropologist from the Florida Department of Community Affairs during two months of fieldwork in the communities of Apalachicola and Eastpoint, on Florida's Gulf Coast. Although the bulk of the examples of maritime traditions mentioned here are taken from Florida, the techniques for documenting cultural resources can be applied and adapted to many other maritime settings.

Many people assisted in the development of this publication: I am grateful to Ormond Loomis, chief of the Bureau of Florida Folklife Programs, for developing the initial concept. Alan Jabbour and Peter T. Bartis, of the American Folklife Center, refined that concept and made helpful suggestions. James Hardin, the Center's editor, charted a safe passage through the tricky waters of the government publishing process with his customary adroitness.

The National Trust for Historic Preservation provided a grant that enabled the project to obtain the consulting services of maritime folklife experts Paula J. Johnson and Janet C. Gilmore. They in turn offered innumerable suggestions to sharpen the focus of the guide.

The staffs of the American Folklife Center and the Bureau of Florida Folklife Programs provided considerable assistance. In particular, Carl Fleischhauer at the Center offered valuable advice about fieldwork techniques, ethics, and cataloging field data, and assisted with the selection of illustrations, and Yvonne Bryant at the Bureau labored long and hard to type the various drafts.

Fieldwork in the Apalachicola area was conducted by Barbara Beauchamp, Ormond Loomis, and Nancy Nusz, all of the Bureau of Florida Folklife Programs, and by Marcus Hepburn of the Florida Department of Community Affairs.

I am grateful to the many residents of the two study areas who generously took the time of talk with me and other project fieldworkers about their maritime heritage, including Cletus Anderson, Kristen Anderson, Deborah Beard, Dennis Butler, Costa Buzier, George Chapel, Dale Davis, Lloyd Davis, Steve Davis, Virginia Duggar, Angelo Fichera, Joe Fichera, Ken Folsom, Royce Hodge, Charles House, Robert Ingle, George Kirvin, Alice and Grady Leavins, John Lee, Nannette Lolley, Woody Miley, Isabel Nichols, Stan Norred, Christo Poloronis, Gloria and Sonny Polous, Willie Polous, Corky Richards, Arthur Ross, Lawrence Sangaray, Lawrence Scarabin, Bud Seymour, Walter Shell, Judy Stokowski-Hall, Willie Speed, Anthony Taranto, Linda Thompson, Andrew Valkuchuk, Ralph Varnes, Louie Van Vleet, Carla Watson, George Wefing, and Donnie Wilson of Apalachicola; Corena and Loys Cain, Buford Golden, James Hewitt, Bernard Miller, Xuripha Miller, Inez and Frank "Sonny Boy" Segree, and Bobby Shiver of Eastpoint; Joan Bouington of St. George Island; Eddie Baker, Albert Gufford, Donald Herrin, Mat Roland, and Raymond Singleton of Mayport; Joann and Charles Herrin, Thomas Herrin, and Camilla "Mickie" McRae of Jacksonville; John Gavagan of Atlantic Beach; and Geraldine Margerum of Neptune Beach.

Charlie Nevells, of Stonington, Maine, and Mack Novack, a native of Eastpoint, Florida, kindly granted permission to quote the lyrics of songs they wrote about commercial fishing.

Joe Halusky, extension agent with the Florida Sea Grant Program, provided helpful information about the commercial and recreational fisheries of northeastern Florida. Helen Cooper Floyd and Hilton

The home, boats, wharf, and gear of fisherman Andrew Gove of Stonington, Maine. Photo copyright © by David Klopfenstein

Floyd, natives of Mayport who now reside in Pascagoula, Mississippi, supplied information and photographs concerning Mayport.

The guide has benefited from the advice of many individuals who attended meetings to review preliminary drafts, including Scott Andree, Florida Sea Grant Program; William Derr, Florida Inland Navigation District; Beth Drabyk, Organized Fishermen of Florida; Rusty Fleetwood, Coastal Heritage Society; Roberta Hammond, Florida Department of Community Affairs; Ann Henderson, Florida Endowment for the Humanities; Lynn Hickerson, National Trust for Historic Preservation; Linda Lampl, T.A. Herbert & Associates; Jim Miller, Bureau of Archaeological Research, Florida Department of State; Joan Morris, Florida Photographic Archives, Florida Department of State; Charles Olsen, Florida Trust for Historic Preservation; J. Anthony Paredes, Florida State University; Charles Thomas, Bureau of Marketing, Florida Department of Natural Resources; William Thurston, Bureau of Historic Preservation, Florida Department of State; Patricia Wickman, Division of Historical Resources, Florida Department of State. Folklorists Robert S. McCarl, Jr., and Gary Stanton provided insightful comments about the manuscript. Any errors contained in this publication are, of course, solely my responsibility.

Finally, I wish to thank my wife, LeeEllen Friedland, for considerable support with all aspects of the project, including fieldwork, cataloging of field data, and editorial assistance.

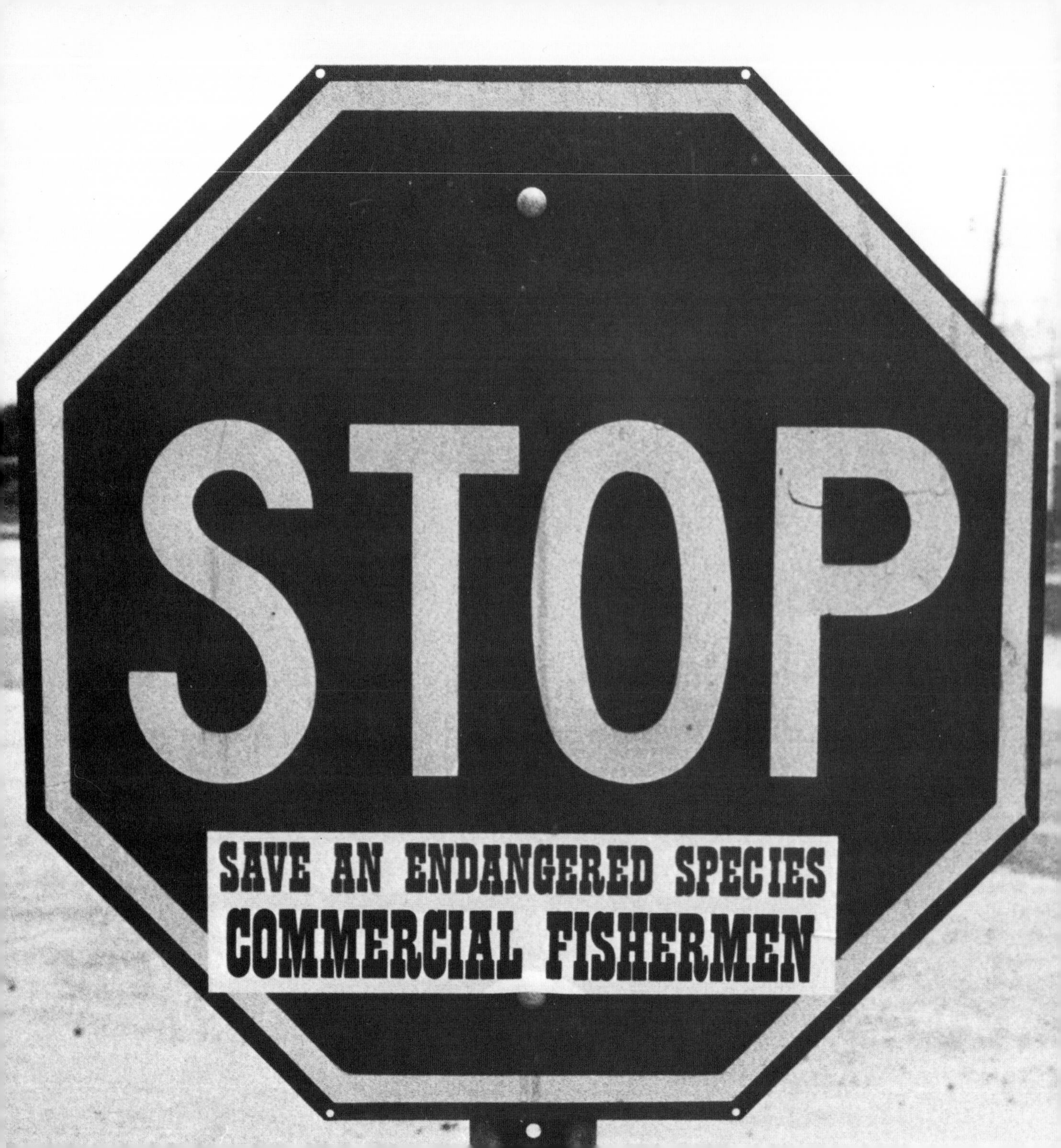
STOP
SAVE AN ENDANGERED SPECIES
COMMERCIAL FISHERMEN

Introduction

During the summer, when I was a youngster, it was common for my parents to take my brother and me on drives from our inland Maine community to the coast. Although these drives were not very long–we lived about forty miles away as the crow flies–the differences in landscape between my home territory and the ocean-dominated coast were striking. And there were many less spectacular differences as well: the way people talked, the food they ate, the jobs they held (notably in commercial fishing and in businesses that catered to tourists), and the rhythms of their daily lives. Eventually, the elementary conclusion entered my young mind that the regular ways of doing things in my family and community were distinct from the regular way of doing things in a maritime community. And, as I was to learn many years later, these were cultural differences.

What is culture? Culture is a complex and ever-changing body of knowledge that provides rules, methods, and beliefs for conducting life within families, communities, and the various occupational, ethnic, religious, recreational, and other human groups. In the course of everyday life, people use cultural knowledge in many forms, including the structure and rules of language, beliefs about nature and the supernatural, and methods for getting and preparing food. Culture also encompasses the range of ideas that define beauty, and how those ideas influence such things as the shape of a boat, the color of paint used on a house, the performance of a song, and the way clothes are hung on a clothesline.

At the heart of the concept of maritime culture is the assumption that the natural environment plays a major role in shaping human behavior and that similar settings are likely to stimulate similar responses. In other words, people living in maritime settings have a maritime way of life, just as people living in mountainous settings have a peculiarly mountain way. This sort of environmental determinism is an oversimplification, however, since differences in climate, natural resources, population density, local culture, and economic systems account for a great diversity in the many communities around the world that can be grouped under the loose categorization maritime. Nonetheless, the terms *maritime culture* and *maritime community* are useful because they call attention to similarities in human behavior that arise from broadly analogous environmental circumstances. For example, while the coastal community

Stop sign adorned with bumper sticker at Empire, Louisiana, expresses a sentiment commonly felt in fishing towns. Photo by Nicholas R. Spitzer. Courtesy of Louisiana Folklife Program

of Beaufort, North Carolina, possesses cultural traits that resemble those of many other southern towns, and traits of American communities in general, it also has traits that specifically link it to other maritime communities in the United States and abroad.

What is a maritime community? That is a difficult question. In a community whose economy is dominated by commercial fishing and other maritime trades, the local culture is full of maritime elements. We might call such a place a classic maritime community. Other communities, however, owing to such factors as the diversity of local economies and the size of populations, may have significant but not predominant maritime-related cultural attributes. Major cities, such as New York, Boston, and San Francisco, whose founding and growth are directly related to their fine harbors, are now so populous and economically diverse that maritime aspects of local culture—though important, distinctive, varied, and of great longevity—are not of a scale that permits them to exert an overwhelming influence. On the other hand, with nearly 89,000 miles of saltwater coastline and innumerable miles of freshwater coastline along lakes, rivers, and streams, one may find throughout the United States an enormous number of communities possessing cultural attributes that have maritime connections.[1]

Cultural expressions are often divided into two broad categories: the tangible (tools, boats, lighthouses, and other physical artifacts) and the intangible (songs about fishing, legends about how an island got its name, systems for navigation based on the use of landmarks, and the like). But, to me, this is a misleading separation. To call a song, a legend, or a navigational system intangible is to imply that they have no importance in people's daily lives. This is clearly not the case. Though they do not have physical substance, they have as much functional and symbolic meaning as boats, lighthouses, and widow's walks. Cultural values are lodged in nonphysical expressions just as much as they are in physical ones.

Sometimes forms of expressive culture are intimately connected to a particular place, such as the annual celebration of maritime heritage held in Apalachicola, Florida, initially known as the Mardi Gras when it began in the early part of this century, and now known as the Seafood Festival. A particularly distinctive element of this tribute to marine resources and occupations is the selection of an oyster king and queen. A grassroots cultural expression that is equally complex and place-specific is the annual International Eelpout Festival held over a winter weekend on Leech Lake in Walker, Minnesota. This event, which was begun by the owner of a local sports shop in 1979, pokes fun at the many fishing contests held in the north by focusing attention on the eelpout, perhaps the least desired fish in Minnesota. The festival is also about turning the seasons topsy-turvy. According to one report: "The pouters spend a lot of their time denying that winter is winter and ice is ice. By sundown on Saturday, two volleyball games are in progress at different encampments. (In past festivals, anglers have held bowling contests using frozen eelpouts for pins.) One team here has built a split-level ice house with sundeck, volleyball court, bowling alley, and golf range."[2]

Sometimes forms of expressive culture underscore connections with other times and places, such as saints' processions enacted in the United States that originated in Europe. For example, every year on or near Santa Rosalia's Day (September 4), Italian-Americans in Monterey, California, reenact a Sicilian tradition that includes carrying a statue of the saint through the streets of the city and then down to the harbor for a blessing of the commercial fishing fleet. Artifacts can also have strong connections to other places. In Tarpon Springs, Florida, a coastal community with a large population of Greek-Americans, the shapes of wooden boats once used in the local sponge industry exhibit characteristic features of the small craft of Greece.[3]

Folklorists are interested in the ways cultural expressions vary over time and from place to place, because variation reveals different solutions to common problems, solutions often inseparable from local contexts. Locally built boats used for fishing in Maine differ from those built and used on Florida's Gulf Coast on the basis of different traditions of design and construction, but also on the basis of differences in environmental conditions. The study of variation within a relatively small area can also help us understand how a body of traditional knowledge changes over time in response to social, economic, and technological factors.

In some cases, expressive culture transcends the local scene and assumes other levels of meaning for a wider audience. For example, a dialectal utterance of Coastal Maine—"a-yuh"—has become a widely recognized symbol of the stereotypic Down Easter and is featured on T-Shirts, postcards, and commercial sound recordings of Maine humor. In other cases, certain local artifacts become invested with deeply symbolic meanings. The magnificent Viking Age craft preserved at the cathedral-like Viking Ships Museum in Oslo (especially the Gokstad ship and the Oseberg ship) have become symbols for Norway's great maritime heritage.

Why do folklorists study expressive culture? They study it because expressive culture emerges from shared experiences and values, and examples of this expression serve as windows to a group's worldview. In other words, they are a means of viewing community life and values from an insider's perspective.

Documenting Maritime Folklife was developed in response to laymen's requests for guidance with the identification and documentation of cultural resources found in maritime communities. It provides guidance for the collection of information on maritime folklife that can be used to teach residents of maritime communities—policy makers and average citizens alike—how to better appreciate both physical and non-physical cultural resources, to assess the significance of these resources, and to develop strategies for their conservation.[4]

---

[1] U.S. Department of Commerce, Bureau of Census. *Statistical Abstract of the United States 1986* (Washington: Department of Commerce, 1986), 200.

[2] Erik Larson, "It Seems Every Fish Has Its Day—Even the Hated Eelpout," *Wall Street Journal*, February 20, 1987, pp. 1, 11.

[3] These vessels are discussed by anthropologist H. Russell Bernard in his article "Greek Sponge Boats in Florida," *Anthropological Quarterly* 38, no. 2 (1965): 41–54.

[4] *Conservation* is deliberately given preference here over *preservation*. In doing so, I follow Hufford's reasoning in distinguishing between the two terms. As she has written, "Preservation arrests the evolution and decay of a barn, a cucumber, or a tract of wilderness. Conservation enhances the potential of a renewable resources, efficiently moving it through a cycle of use, renewal and re-use. Conservation entails careful attention to the co-evolving features within a system." (Mary Hufford, *One Space, Many Places: Folklife and Land Use in New Jersey's Pinlands National Reserve* (Washington: Library of Congress, 1986), 107–8.

Part 1: What to Document

To give the reader a sense of the form and variety of traditions found in maritime communities, this section provides a few typical examples. While such a listing emphasizes separate categories or genres, it is important to remember that the traditional expressions always take place within the live cultural settings that create them. Jokes, beliefs about luck, and boat types can only be understood within their natural contexts. And within such natural contexts several traditional expressions may be enacted at the same time. When a commercial fisherman pilots a locally built boat to fishing grounds by lining up "marks" (landmarks), at the same time interpreting the circular flight patterns of sea gulls as a sign of an impending storm, traditional knowledge about boat forms suited to local conditions, navigation by eye, and prediction of weather are integrated.

In maritime communities, one rich context for traditional expressions is the occupational group. Commercial fishermen, fish plant workers, boat builders, net makers, harbor pilots, and deep-sea fishing boat captains all acquire an amazing variety of traditional knowledge from coworkers that they pass along to others in the workplace.

At the core of any occupation is the technique required to perform a given task.[1]

This technique consists of the ways workers use their tools, respond to their environment, and interact with other workers. For example, the central technique of oyster-shucking consists of four operations: breaking off the tip of the oyster, inserting a knife blade in the shell, cutting the muscle from the top and bottom of the shell, and depositing the meat into a bucket. To outsiders this may sound like a fairly simple procedure, but insiders know that skillful execution of the sequence of movements takes years of practice. Virginia Duggar of Apalachicola, Florida, is an oyster shucker with over twenty years of experience. Her description of the work conveys its complexity.

You used to use a hammer and an iron block with a tip-thing on it. And you hold the oyster behind the block with the lip of the oyster on this raised-up piece and you hit across that thin part of the oyster with the hammer. We have shucking hammers which are flat on both sides. And the main thing is to keep the point of your knife up towards the top shell. Now, you have a top and a bottom to an oyster. Ninety percent of the time the top of the oyster will be flatter, and bottom of the oyster will be rounder. So, you keep your knife, the point of your knife, and you bring it across that top shell. And then you put the top shell

Hands of oyster shucker. Photo by Lyntha Eiler. Courtesy of Calvert Marine Museum

off, and then you come under and you cut off the bottom of the eye of the bottom shell. But if you're not particular to keep that knife kind of pushed up against the top of that top shell, then you'll cut your oyster. Your knife will go right through the belly part of it.[2]

Surrounding the central technique of an occupation are many related expressive forms: words and gestures used between workers, the arrangement of tools and other objects within the work area, and customs practiced there. In the oyster house, the shuckers select oyster knives with the most appropriate blades for certain shell shapes; distinguish oysters of varying size, shape, color, and shell composition; tell stories about events that have occurred in the oyster house; gesture to the "houseman" to bring more oysters; and, perhaps, organize a party for another shucker who is about to be married. Examined altogether, these traditional activities help reveal how the group of shuckers expresses itself and its values.[3]

Frequently, certain kinds of traditional knowledge are shared only by the members of a particular occupation: the names and locations of shrimp fishing grounds are often known only by the shrimp fishermen within a specific area. Other kinds of knowledge, such as environmental clues used to predict the weather, might be known by persons in several occupations or by the community at large. A prominent example of traditional knowledge used by boat operators from different occupational groups relates to navigation. Although state-of-the-art electronic navigation devices are available to contemporary commercial fisher-

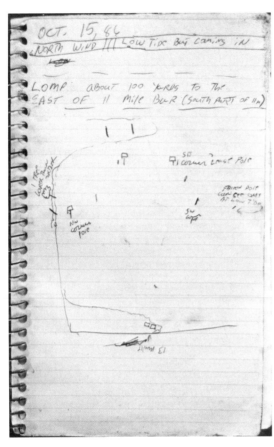

Page from the "range book" of oysterman Ken Folsom of Apalachicola, Florida. Fishermen often use sketches such as these to relocate navigation channels and productive fishing areas. On this page, Folsom has sketched the locations of trees, points of land, and poles marking the boundaries of a leased oyster bed—some of which he'll line up in order to find a course to a "lump" of marketable oysters he discovered on a previous trip. Photo by David A. Taylor (FMP86–BDT025/12)

tiating narrow, tricky passages and avoiding underwater obstructions that can damage boats and fishing gear. Sometimes skippers will record this information in notebooks; more often, they will memorize it.[4] Although this basic system of navigation is well known to many boatmen, the courses themselves are usually known only by those who travel the waters of a specific region. Sometimes, as in the case of marks used to locate a rich fishing ground, courses are closely guarded secrets known only to a few. In any case, systems of navigation are worthy of researchers' attention because of their historic importance to maritime peoples, and also because they can provide insight into the ways watermen conceptualize space above and below the water.[5]

Although all folklife expression is embedded in a larger context, for the purpose of documentation and study it is useful to analyze them by category. Several of the most common ones are: oral traditions, beliefs, customs, material culture, and foodways.

Oral Traditions

Oral traditions include jokes, riddles, rhymes, legends, songs, and stories, as well as non-narrative forms such as jargon, regional speech, and local place names. Often these expressions can be distinguished from normal discourse on the basis of certain verbal clues, or "markers," that announce the beginning of an oral performance. For example, the phrase "that reminds me of the one about . . ." suggests that a joke is about to be told. "As the old people used to say . . ." may herald a proverb. Tall tales, on the other hand, may not be identifiable at first, but gradually

men and other boat operators, many who operate close to shore still calculate a straight-line course using a time-honored system based on lining up two landmarks. A fisherman might plot his course to a prime fishing spot by aligning a familiar tree with the steeple of the local church. A line, or "range," such as this helps captains locate fishing spots, and also assists them in negotiating

define themselves as the teller begins to exaggerate. John Gavagan of Atlantic Beach, Florida, relates a brief tall tale:

[My friend] told me that he remembered when there wasn't any mullet. He said there was a big drought about fishing and the beach fishermen stayed there [on the beach] all winter and [got] nothing whatsoever. They would actually go in their boats and go looking [for fish]. He said that they saw a fire one night on the very far end of the little jetties. And they pulled in there to see maybe if they were catching something. And [they] saw that there were two porpoises there roasting a possum. That's how bad the fishing was. You know that's bad.[6]

Sometimes an oral performance can be very brief and can occur with no warning at all. In the following interchange, the interviewer falls for a verbal trap set by Mayport, Florida, net maker and former shrimper Martin Cooper:

Interviewer: What's the most important part of [catching shrimp]?

Cooper: The most important part is, I'll explain it to you this way. The shrimping operation starts at the bow stem of a boat and it ends where you tie the cod end. If anything goes wrong in between any of them places it affects your shrimping. And, ah, but the most important thing, getting back to your question. What is the thing that holds the steering wheel on? You know, that, what's that little thing you screw on behind the steering wheel to hold it on?

Interviewer: A nut or something?

Cooper: That's right, *the nut behind the wheel* is the most important thing.[7]

Personal-experience stories and legends are other narrative forms. Personal experience stories are stories that recount especially dramatic episodes in people's lives. Turning an account of an experience into art, the storyteller frames it with a beginning, middle, and end, and peoples it with a cast of characters.

Captain Eddie Baker of Mayport, Florida, a retired shrimp fisherman, relates the following personal-experience story about a close call:

Baker: I've got in trouble in a storm. I got caught down on the beach here in a storm when everybody [else] went with the weather, and I figured I could have beat [against] the weather to St. Augustine. And it took me, well, it took me nineteen hours.

Interviewer: Going right into the wind?

Baker: Going into the wind. And I had to slow down, and something tell me, "You slow it down." And I slowed the boat down. And then, the boy right there said, "Captain, you got the boat full of water." I said, "It is?" I said, "Ease the anchor overboard." And he got down in the hold, and all the trash, all the trash [had] got in the pump. And [he had to] clean it out . . . . I let the engine run, and he pumped it out. We got the anchor up, and we made it on to St. Augustine. We got to St. Augustine, and he said, "Captain, you can't go in there." And I said, "You do like I tell you to do." I say, "I'm not up here by myself." And I set the compass and went straight in [to] the bar with two other fellow's boats behind me. And I got on in [by] the bar, and they said, "Hey, you going to Augustine?" And I said, "No, I'm going on home." I come up through the inside [passage], come on in to Mayport. And I got inside, and I said, "Thank you, Jesus."[8]

Retired shrimp boat captain Eddie Baker (right) of Mayport, Florida, discusses his career with fieldworker David Taylor. The last vessel Baker skippered, the Miss Alice *(named after Baker's wife), is seen in the background. Photo by Frank Smith. Courtesy of Florida Publishing Co.*

Legends are narratives, supposedly based on fact, that are told about persons, places, or events. For example, in the adjacent fishing communities of Beals and Jonesport, Maine, legends about fisherman Barney Beal are well known. Beal was a giant of a man and the stories about him invariably focus on his tremendous strength. As the stories were passed on to newer generations in the years since Beal's death in 1899, actual events have been embellished and new stories created. In 1956, folklorist Richard Dorson collected this story about Beal from one of Beal's grandsons:

Dorson: Now, you were telling me a very interesting account of the time the bully of Peak's Island challenged him to a fight.

Esten Beal: Yes, I've heard that story told many a time, that he went into Peak's Island to get water for his fishing vessel. And the bully of Peak's Island met him on the beach and challenged him to a fight. So he told him that as soon as he filled his water barrel why he would accommodate him. So he went and filled his water barrel. And they used to use these large molasses tierces for water barrels. So he brought the water barrel down on the beach, and he said, "Well," he said, "I guess

5

before we start, I'll have a drink of water." So he picked up the water barrel and took a drink out of the bunghole, set it down on the beach, and the bully of Peak's Island walked up, slapped him on the shoulder, and says, "Mr. Beal, I don't think I'll have anything to do with you whatever."[9]

Oral traditions common to maritime communities include legends about buried treasure, how an individual met his death at sea, and how an island or some other feature of the landscape acquired its name. Tall tales are frequently told about large or unusual catches of fish, bad weather, and feats of strength. Personal-experience stories abound and are often concerned with such topics as the biggest catch ever made, the strangest catch ever made, and the closest encounter with death on the water.

The vernacular names used for familiar things such as fish, plants, birds, cloud forms, boats, and gear are important elements of traditional knowledge that are expressed orally. While identical terms are sometimes used in different communities, there is generally a good deal of regional variation as well. For example, the end of a trawl net is usually called the "cod end" by New England fishermen, while in the Southeast it is often called the "tail bag." And, not surprisingly, things found only within relatively small geographic regions, including unique boat types or species of fish or birds, possess traditional names unknown outside the region. An example is the "bird dog" boat, an open, inshore fishing craft used along the Gulf Coast of Florida. In many communities, residents follow traditional rules for giving formal names to individual boats. For example, in a large number of fishing towns it is custom-

Net maker Martin Floyd of Mayport, Florida, repairs a shrimp trawl for a local fisherman. Photo by David A. Taylor. Courtesy of Bureau of Florida Folklife Programs

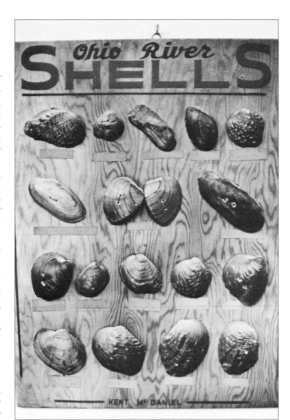

The richness of localized naming practices is epitomized by this display of Ohio River shells. Kent McDaniel of Metropolis, Illinois, submitted the display as his entry in a high school science fair. The names of the shells are as follows:
Row 1 (top, left to right): buckhorn, buzzard-head, rabbit's foot, mule-ear, monkey face
Row 2: yellow buckhorn, butterfly, stock sandshell
Row 3: niggerhead, eggshell, bullhead, pimple back, pigtoe.
Row 4: pocketbook, maple-leaf, three-ridge, wash-board
Photo by Jens Lund

Nearly every maritime occupation has its own jargon of words and phrases, seldom known outside of the occupation, that label fishing gear, tools, procedures, and occupational roles. Place names are of great significance, especially traditional names for fishing grounds. If these names have been in use long enough, they sometimes become recognized as official names and are used on charts. Many, however, are known only by fishermen. Other important names identify local landmarks used for lining up courses and for judging distances along the shore. Names that shrimpers use for landmarks south of Mayport, Florida, followed by the features from which the names were derived, include:

"Crazy House": a shoreside house built to an unorthodox design.

"Golf Ball": a water tower shaped like an enormous golf ball.

"The Road": a dirt road running perpendicular to the shore.

"Three Houses": a cluster of three houses.

Place names like these sometimes continue to be used after the original landmarks have disappeared.

Song is another category of oral expression, and songs with maritime themes or songs performed within the contexts of maritime occupations are sometimes encountered. In the past, songs about the sea and worksongs sung to facilitate certain tasks figured prominently in the lives of seamen and other inhabitants of coastal communities. Today, largely because of technological change in maritime occupations and the spread of popular music through electronic media, these expres-

ary to name a boat after the owner's wife, child, or some other close relative.

The use of distinctive words and phrases also constitutes traditional knowledge expressed orally. In many Florida fishing communities, it is common to hear fishermen use such regionally distinctive words as "hang" (an underwater obstruction), "kicker" (an outboard motor), and "lick" (a pass over fishing grounds with a net or other gear).

sions are less common. For example, with the advent of engines to haul anchors and nets, the need to sing songs that helped concentrate group labor was eliminated. And in most oyster houses, popular music broadcast from a radio has replaced the singing of songs by shuckers, songs sung to reduce the monotony of the work.[10] But residents of maritime communities still compose songs that reflect ties to maritime heritage and associated values. Take, for example, the song "Oyster Man Blues," written by Mack Novak, a native of Eastpoint, Florida.

This song is noteworthy because, in addition to choosing the most distinctive fishery of the Apalachicola Bay region as its theme, it describes oystering from an insider's perspective. It depicts a typical day of oystering, using occupational jargon such as "hickory sticks" (wooden oyster tongs), "cull iron" (metal tool used to bang apart oysters that have formed clumps), "grouper trooper" (state fisheries patrol officer), and "oyster ruler" (measuring device used to determine if oysters are of legal size). Songs like "Oysterman's Blues" can provide researchers with valuable clues to the way insiders conceptualize the process of work, and can help illuminate the values that are important to fishermen, their families, and other residents of their communities.[12]

Beliefs

Beliefs are easily among the most distinctive and enduring portions of maritime culture. Traditional beliefs (popularly called superstitions) are convictions that are usually related to causes and effects and are often manifest in certain practices. Com-

"Oyster Man Blues"

By Mack Novak[11]

[Spoken:]
Now, this is going to be a quick story in oystering in which you have to go out and separate the little oysters from the big oysters so you won't get a ticket. And it goes something like this:

[Sung:]
Their day it starts at 5 A.M.—they hit the bar.
They've got their Maxwell House Coffee in a Bama Mayonnaise jar.
Out goes the anchor, and then over go the tongs.
At 10 A.M. they're saying, "Oh, Lord, where did I go wrong?"

He's got those oysterman's blues.
He can't afford a pair of shoes.
His hickory sticks, well, they're slapping out a tune.
And it's called those oysterman's blues.

When he tongs up those oysters, then he throws them on the deck,
He reaches over to his wife and he gives her a little peck.
Then he hands her a glove and a cull iron,
And says, "Honey, separate these things 'cause I sure am tired."

I've got those oysterman's blues.
I can't afford a pair of shoes.
My hickory sticks, well, they're slapping out a tune
And it's called those oysterman's blues.

[Instrumental Break]

He comes in from the bar expecting to go home,
but there's a grouper trooper on the dock in his grey uniform.
He pulls out his oyster ruler and he goes to work.
When the count is 35 percent, he says, "Hey, you're out of luck."

You've got those oysterman's blues.
You can't afford a pair of shoes.
Your hickory sticks, I'll bet they're slapping out a tune.
And I'll bet it's called those oysterman's blues.

Yeah, it's called those oysterman's blues.

Shrimper Charles Herrin of Jacksonville, Florida, in the pilot house of his fishing boat, Miss Joann. *Photo by David A. Taylor (FMP86–BDT005/28)*

mon examples include beliefs about good and bad luck, signs for predicting the weather, interpretations of supernatural happenings, and remedies for sickness and injury.

Since maritime occupations often place workers in a highly unpredictable, constantly changing, and hazardous environment, it is not surprising that workers hold many beliefs about fortune and misfortune.[13] A primary function of such beliefs is to explain the unexplainable. Watermen generally can cite many actions that invite bad luck. These actions include uttering certain words while aboard a boat, taking certain objects or people on a boat, going out in a boat on a certain day, manipulating parts of a boat in a certain way, or painting boats with certain colors. A Florida shrimp fisherman notes beliefs about bad luck that he and his peers have learned:

> There are a lot of words, you know, that you don't say on a boat. [Like] *alligator.* You don't say *alligator* on a boat or you're going to have a pile of bad luck. You don't have no shells on there, no shells on a boat. You don't turn the

9

hatch cover all the way upside down. You don't carry no black suitcase on no boat. You don't whistle.[14]

Many beliefs about bad luck have been part of local maritime culture for so long that their origins are unknown. Occasionally, however, stories are told that either describe the origin of a belief or depict an instance where circumstances appear to validate one. The following is an example of the latter:

The shell story, now. In fact, this boy used to work with me on the *Miss Virgie*. He was out there dragging [for shrimp] one night, and he was on the stern, and he hung up [his net]. So, he run up there, and cut the engine down, and it took him a while to get off the hang. And he started dragging again. The engine shut off. So, he got that going again, started dragging some more, picked up [his net], and went on the stern, and [was] helping his crew pick out [shrimp], and he noticed the boat started to go around one way, and he started running for the pilot house. And the [automatic] pilot had hung up. It carried the boat around one side, and when the quadrant was supposed to stop the rudder in the back, well, it did stop the rudder, but the pilot didn't stop. So, it tore up part of the dash, and ripped all the pilot out of the floor. And this is all in one night. So, he kind of, he believes in all of that kind of stuff pretty much, so he said, "There's something on this boat that isn't supposed to be on it." So, he got to looking and he hunted all over the boat. And he got on top of the pilot house, and there was a line of shells on the pilot house that his deck hand had put up there to dry off good. And he said, "Them shells was the reason we had all the trouble." He threw them shells overboard, and he went for months, never had any more trouble.[15]

Beliefs about actions that invite good luck appear to be fewer in number than those about bad luck, but many can be found. Beliefs about good luck include the breaking of a bottle of champagne or other liquid over the bow of a vessel when it is launched, participating in a blessing-of-the-fleet ceremony, placing a coin under a mast, carrying a lucky object aboard a boat, and stepping on or off a boat with the same foot.

Beliefs about the prediction of weather and the movement of fish are usually quite numerous. These beliefs, often linked to the detection of minute environmental changes, reflect watermen's intimate contact with the natural environment. A retired Florida shrimp fisherman recalled:

> When you were shrimping and you started catching shrimp with their legs just blood-red, you knew to watch very close because you were fixing to have either a strong northeaster or a strong southeaster. Their legs will turn just as red as fire, so, yes, their legs will turn just as red as fire, and you know you're in for a spell of bad weather.[16]

Another shrimper who fishes out of the same community explained how wind direction can provide clues about the location of shrimp:

> There's certain places that shrimp get in in different types of weather. Say, for instance, you go out to the jetties one morning, and it's blowing a pretty stiff southwest wind. Well, that tells you, in most cases, that you want to go southwest on the beach, get close up to the beach, and you probably would do better. If you come out of the jetties, and it's blowing a pretty good, stiff northeast wind, you can go northeast or southeast, but you want to go offshore in the deep water, and most of the time

you'll do better that way. When the wind is blowing out of the northwest, turn your boat back around, and go back to the dock, and make you another cup of coffee because you ain't going to catch a thing. It just dries it up completely. A northwest wind is a bad wind on shrimping. I don't know why, but you just don't catch no shrimp.[17]

Sometimes beliefs are expressed concisely in the form of a rhyme. When discussing the relationship between wind direction and fishing success, an oysterman from Apalachicola, Florida, remarked to a researcher:

> East is the least,
> and the west is the best.[18]

In other words, in Apalachicola Bay, winds out of the east generally produce conditions that are least conducive to good catches, while winds out of the west tend to favor good catches. Other "signs" often associated with weather prediction include rings around the moon, concentrations of refracted sunlight in the sky called "sundogs," the color of the sky at sunrise and sunset, and the color and texture of the sea.

Beliefs related to the supernatural are also found in maritime communities: ghosts, phantom ships, burning ships, or sea monsters. But, because many people are reluctant to discuss them, they are considerably less conspicuous than beliefs about luck and weather. A net maker tells of his experience with a supernatural event:

> I saw an occurrence, and I never said very much about it. . . . It was in the bay, and it never really got close enough for me to really see it, but it was right down off town, off straight out from the city marina. And I watched it come in from the Gulf. And it come in and went across a bar where it's

Breaking a bottle of champagne over the bow of a new vessel at its launching is a widely practiced custom believed to invoke good luck. Here the Chesapeake Bay skipjack Connie Francis *is christened at Piney Point, Maryland, by Connie Goddard, wife of the boat's builder, Francis Goddard. Photo by Carl Fleischhauer. Courtesy of Calvert Marine Museum*

11

shallow. Ain't no way a ship that big could cross it. And it appeared to be a big schooner-type, a big sailing ship of some type. And to me, there was no explaining it away. It was a ship come in there and went across that bar. But I don't know what it was. And I was curious about it, but I never said much about it because people will say, "Oh, you're crazy." So, you just don't talk about it. But this vessel come in from the old pass, just like it would have done a hundred years ago. And it come in and it crossed Courtney Point, and Courtney Point is too shallow. And when it crossed it went behind the day marker, and still went right on up the bay towards St. Andrews. And then it just wasn't there.[19]

Customs

Customs are similar to beliefs in that they involve verbal and nonverbal expressions that are put into play under certain circumstances. Unlike beliefs, they are not primarily concerned with assumptions that certain signs or actions will indicate or cause particular results. Customs are practices followed as a matter of course. Well-known customs are associated with holidays and festivals, as well as rites of passage such as birth, marriage, entry into an occupation, retirement, and death. Frequently, important events include a variety of customary practices. Weddings, for example, feature such things as traditional vows, music, clothing, rice throwing, food, drink, toasts, dancing, bouquet and garter tossing, and car "sabotaging." These customs are arranged in a specific order that is well known to everyone in the community.

Many customs are unique to maritime communities, although some are carried on in connection with major holidays. In several of Maine's coastal communities, lobster

boat races, rowboat races, and the sale of seafood prepared in a traditional manner are key elements of annual Fourth of July celebrations. At Easter time in many coastal regions of the country, local clergymen bless boats and their crews as they pass by in a procession. Community-based seafood festivals also include many customs. In the town of Apalachicola, Florida, site of one of the nation's most productive oyster fisheries, an annual festival is held to celebrate local maritime heritage. Inaugurated in 1915, the festival includes such events as the crowning of King Retsyo ("oyster" spelled backwards), a blessing of the fleet, an oyster-shucking contest, an oyster-eating contest, crab races, and the sale of local seafood.

Customs related to death also have maritime correlatives. They include memorial services held at sea for fishermen lost there, and tombstones that display engravings of boats, anchors, and other nautical objects.

Finally, there are remedies for sickness, especially seasickness, and injury. For many commercial fishermen, wounds caused by sharp fish fins are a constant hazard. The following is a description of a method used by some fishermen to ease the pain caused by such injuries:

> Take a penny and wrap it in a piece of bacon and put it on [the wound]. And whether it be a nail or a catfish puncture, . . . you will not believe what it will do. . . . I've personally, a number of times, took the penny and a slice of bacon about this big and put the penny inside of it, and just fold it over, put it right to the puncture wound. And you will not believe. The next day it's like nothing ever happened to you.[20]

Material Culture

Material culture refers to artifacts and the knowledge required for their creation and use. These artifacts are usually the most easily identifiable forms of traditional expression. In maritime communities, boats of all sizes and types--from small plywood row boats to large shrimp trawlers--are extremely important elements of the cultural environment. In communities where builders design and construct watercraft according to informal rules and procedures handed down over the years, boats reflect builders' evolving solutions to such problems as depth of water, prevailing winds, climate, availability of construction materials, and intended uses. Due to gradual improvement over time, many boats, such as the Apalachicola Bay oyster skiff and the Maine lobster boat, are superbly suited to local contexts.

Fishing gear is another rich and significant aspect of maritime material culture. Nets, traps, buoys, line trawls, spears, cane poles, hooks, lures, anchors, weights, sinkers, bait bags, and other types of equipment illustrate the methods fishermen have developed for capturing local marine species. As with boats, fishing gear often undergoes change over time in response to local conditions and materials.

Shoreside buildings of all kinds, such as houses, boat shops, boat houses, net lofts, shucking houses, and fish camps, represent a third major category of maritime material culture. Such structures often illustrate the adaptation of traditional design and construction techniques to a maritime environment. They also reveal local preferences about the arrangement of interior space,

In the fishing community of Apalachicola, Florida, residents annually celebrate their maritime heritage with a seafood festival. An important element of this festival, which dates back to early years of the twentieth century, is the crowning of King Retsyo (oyster spelled backwards) and a festival queen. In 1986, Lori Ingram was chosen festival queen and Bob Jones was selected to serve as King Retsyo. Photo by LeeEllen Friedland (FMP86–BLF001/30)

The repair and manufacture of fishing gear is a common activity in maritime communities. Sometimes the work is carried on by specialists, such as oyster tong maker Corky Richards of Apalachicola, Florida (shown here); sometimes it is done by the fishermen themselves or other nonspecialists. Photo by David A. Taylor (FMP86–BDT027/16)

and the spatial requirements of traditional activities such as oyster shucking, net making, and boat building. How the interiors of dwellings are arranged–the shapes, sizes, and locations of rooms and the type and placement of furnishings–says much about the traditional patterns people use to order their lives.

In addition to boats, fishing gear, and buildings, many other artifacts illustrate a community's relationship to maritime culture. Thus, decoys and blinds are used for hunting waterfowl; specific types of boots, caps, and other items of clothing are worn by commercial fishermen; and yard decorations consist of overtly maritime objects

such as salvaged anchors, ship wheels, hawsers, and shells. Artifacts also include wharves and moorings, paintings and signs, half-hull boat models used by builders to develop hull designs, and full-rigged scale models used to decorate interiors of homes or restaurants. All these items, from the fishing vessel to the painting of a lighthouse on a mailbox, can reveal much about maritime culture when viewed in relationship to other objects and human activities.

Foodways

Foodways are the traditions associated with the growing, gathering, preparation, serving, and consumption of food. In mar-

Locally caught seafood usually plays a major role in the food traditions of maritime communities. Here members of a Beaux Bridge, Louisiana, family prepare a crawfish "boil." In southern Louisiana, the consumption of crawfish caught in the Atchafalaya Basin is the centerpiece of many social gatherings for family members and friends. Photo by Nicholas R. Spitzer. Courtesy of Louisiana Folklife Program

itime communities many food traditions are based on locally available fish and shellfish. For example, residents of Key West, Florida, have developed several unique recipes for the preparation of conch, a shellfish that was extremely abundant in local waters in the past and served as a major food source during the Depression.[21] Some recipes are unique to certain areas. For example, in the fishing communities of Newfoundland battered and fried tongues of codfish are considered a delicacy, and in parts of coastal Virginia "planked" shad is a specialty. Much regional variation appears in the names for local fish and shellfish, the types of food served in combination with fish and shellfish, and taboos against eating certain types of fish and shellfish. Foodways also play a role in traditional rituals and celebrations. In fact, food can be the keystone of an entire event. In the New England clambake, frequently held in connection with family reunions, participants gather at the seashore and build a large wood fire that is allowed to burn down to coals. Next, a feast of local clams, lobsters, and corn on the cob is steamed over the coals between layers of seaweed. Other events involving foods include boat-launching ceremonies and seafood festivals. In these contexts, as with the clambake, foodways occur with many other traditional expressions.

---

[1] The concept of occupational technique is developed by Robert S. McCarl, Jr., in his essay "Occupational Folklife: A Theoretical Hypothesis," in *Working Americans: Contemporary Approaches to Occupational Folklife,* edited by Robert H. Byington, Smithsonian Folklife Series, no. 3 (Los Angeles: California Folklore Society, 1978), 318.

[2] Interview with oyster shucker Virginia Duggar of Apalachicola, Florida, recorded October 10, 1986, by David Taylor. On deposit at Florida Folklife Archives, Bureau of Florida Folklife Programs, White Springs, Florida.

[3] For a fine description of the expressive dimension of oyster shucking, see: Paula J. Johnson, "'Sloppy Work for Women': Shucking Oysters on the Patuxent." In *Working the Water: The Commercial Fisheries of Maryland's Patuxent River,* edited by Paula J. Johnson (Charlottesville: The University Press of Virginia, 1988), 35–51.

[4] For illustrations of this process, see: Hufford, *One Space, Many Places,* 58; Gary R. Butler, "Culture, Cognition, and Communication: Fishermen's Location Finding in L'Anse-a-Canards, Newfoundland," *Canadian Folklore Canadien* 5, nos. 1–2 (1983): 7–21, and Shepard Forman, "Cognition and The Catch: The Location of Fishing Spots in a Brazilian Coastal Village," *Ethnology* 6, no. 4 (1967): 417–26.

[5] Anthropological studies of traditional systems of navigation include: Richard Feinberg, *Polynesian Seafaring and Navigation: Ocean Travel in Anutan Culture and Society* (Kent, Ohio, and London: The Kent State University Press, 1988); Thomas Gladwin, *East is a Big Bird: Navigation and Logic on Puluwat Atoll* (Cambridge: Harvard University Press, 1970); and David Lewis, *We, the Navigators* (Honolulu: The University Press of Hawaii, 1972).

[6] Interview with John Gavagan of Neptune Beach, Florida, recorded July 26, 1986, by David Taylor. On deposit at the Florida Folklife Archives, Bureau of Florida Folklife Programs, White Springs, Florida.

[7] Interview with net maker Martin Cooper of Mayport, Florida, recorded July 27, 1984, by David Taylor. Florida Folklife Archives accession number C–86–198.

[8] Interview with retired shrimp fisherman Eddie Baker of Mayport, Florida, recorded July 16, 1986, by David Taylor. On deposit at the Florida Folklife Archives, White Springs, Florida. For a fine compilation of personal experience narratives concerned with a maritime occupation, see: Timothy C. Lloyd and Patrick B. Mullen, *Lake Erie Fishermen: Work, Tradition, and Identity* (Urbana and Chicago: University of Illinois Press, 1990).

[9] Richard Dorson, *Buying the Wind* (Chicago: University of Chicago Press, 1964), 50–51. For other stories about Beal, see: Velton Peabody, *Tall Barney: The Giant*

Billy Payne (left) and Henry Overton prepare to do some recreational fishing on Georgia's Alapaha River, aboard Payne's home-made boat. Photo by David Stanley (4–17534/24)

of Beals Island (Williamsville, N.Y.: Periwinkle Press, 1975).

[10] In shucking houses where the use of electric shucking machines has replaced shucking by hand, the noise level created by the machines is so high that singing is virtually unintelligible. In such contexts, shuckers often listen to a radio that broadcasts music throughout the room, or to personal radios or cassette players they listen to through headphones. Singing by oyster shuckers is discussed by Johnson in her article " 'Sloppy Work for Women': Shucking Oysters on the Patuxent," 49–51.

[11] Mack Novak, "Oysterman's Blues," St. George Sound Records CSS–152, 1978. 45 r.p.m. disk recording. Copyright Mack Novak, reprinted with permission.

[12] For a more detailed analysis, see: David A. Taylor, "Songs About Fishing: Examples of Contemporary Maritime Songs," *Canadian Folklore Canadien 12, no.2 (1990):* 85–99.

[13] Commercial fishing is considered the most hazardous of all industrial occupations in the United States. Statistics show that fishermen are seven times more likely to die on the job than workers in the next most dangerous occupation.

[14] Interview with shrimp fisherman Charles Herrin of Jacksonville, Florida, recorded July 31, 1986, by

David Taylor. Tape recorded interview on deposit at the Florida Folklife Archives, White Springs, Florida.

[15] Interview with shrimp fisherman Charles Herrin of Jacksonville, Florida, recorded July 31, 1986, by David Taylor.

[16] Interview with retired fisherman Albert Gufford of Mayport, Florida, recorded August 8, 1986, by David Taylor. On deposit at the Florida Folklife Archives, White Springs, Florida.

[17] Interview with shrimp fisherman Charles Herrin of Jacksonville, Florida, recorded July 31, 1986, by David Taylor.

[18] From oyster fisherman Cletus Anderson of Apalachicola, Florida. Recorded in fieldnotes by Nancy Nusz and David Taylor on November 6, 1986. Notes on deposit at the Florida Folklife Archives, White Springs, Florida.

[19] Net maker Jimmy Carden of Panama City, Florida, in the video documentary *Fishing All My Days* (White Springs: Bureau of Florida Folklife Programs, 1985).

[20] Interview with John Gavagan of Neptune Beach, Florida, recorded July 26, 1986, by David Taylor.

[21] In addition to playing an important role in local foodways, conch serves a symbolic function. For most Floridians, the term *conch* denotes a native of the Keys.

Part 2: How to Document

Researchers can draw upon a core of techniques to document the variety of cultural expressions described in the preceding chapter. Cultural specialists, like doctors, lawyers, and cabinet makers, employ a professional methodology, and the results of their endeavors are judged according to certain professional standards. Skillful execution of techniques will not only result in the collection of information of high quality but will implicitly show respect for the people being documented. Since Part 2 provides only a general introduction to documentation, readers are advised to consult works contained in the bibliography for more detailed information.

The Project Plan

The first step in any project to document maritime cultural resources is the formulation of a plan that addresses certain basic questions about the work to be undertaken, including:

1. What are the goals of the project?
2. What are the boundaries of the study area?
3. What methods are to be used to collect data?
4. Who will be involved with the project and what tasks will they be assigned?
5. What equipment and supplies will be required?
6. What funds must be obtained?
7. What is the project's timetable?
8. How will field data be organized and preserved after the project has been completed?
9. What cultural specialists and institutions, if any, are to be involved?
10. How will the public be informed about the project?
11. How will the public be involved with the project?
12. What products will be developed with the collected data?

Even though aspects of the plan may change over the course of the project, much time and effort will be saved and confusion avoided if the answers to as many of these questions as possible are determined before other project activities commence.[1]

Projects can be conducted at various levels of depth and extent, depending on a number of factors, including the needs of the project, available time and resources, and the expertise of personnel. One project might attempt to survey a community's expressive culture comprehensively. Another might seek to document one type of cultural expression, such as net-making skills or architecture. Yet another might document a single, local boat type.

If the project is to be a group effort, a project coordinator should be selected. The coordinator will determine the assignment of tasks in accordance with fieldworkers' specific knowledge or interests, or along the lines of the study area's demographic or geographic features. The coordinator may also decide if project participants are to work singly, in pairs, or in teams.

Cultural institutions such as historical societies, museums, libraries, and archives can enhance the success of a project in a number of ways. In addition to providing access to their collections, they can often supply technical assistance concerning methods for collecting, cataloging, and preserving field data. Some repositories lend tape recorders, cameras, and other field equipment. Choose a suitable repository to ensure the preservation of field data long after the project has ended. Making the selection at the start of the project will allow fieldworkers to comply with any special requirements and procedures established by the repository. For example, if cataloging procedures require that all photographs be accompanied by specific data (such as date, subject, place of the photograph, and name of the photographer), fieldworkers will be prepared to record these data when the photograph is taken. Many repositories have forms that can be used by fieldworkers for collecting and cataloging field data, and for the acceptance of donated materials.

The goal of a project might be to document some aspect of an area's maritime heritage and preserve the documents in an archive. Alternatively, a project's goal might include not only collection and preservation of data but also dissemination of portions of it. There are many ways to inform others about local maritime heritage. One can plan exhibits, walking tours, or presentations of maritime skills at public schools in conjunction with the study of local history. One can arrange a local maritime folk arts day consisting of demonstrations of a variety of traditional skills such as boatbuilding, net-making, oyster-shucking, storytelling, and cooking. Possible publications include local histories, cook books, photo albums, and anthologies of local tales.

The development of such projects requires careful planning and, in some cases, budgeting. If funds are necessary, it may be appropriate to solicit contributions from local businesses and organizations. If a project requires major funding, investigate possible resources, including granting institutions, locally based corporations, and foundations.[2] Local or state arts councils, state humanities councils, state historic preservation offices, municipal offices of cultural affairs, and state folk cultural offices can sometimes provide funding and/or information about grant programs sponsored by other agencies.

Preliminary Research

In order to obtain maximum benefit from time in the field, the researcher must locate and analyze as much information as possible about the study area and the topics the project addresses before the start of fieldwork. If significant data are uncovered, they can help determine the best course for fieldwork and enhance the quality of work in the field. To ensure that research efforts

Historic photographs are a valuable source of data. This photo from the Florida Photographic Archive depicts a parade held in conjunction with the 1915 Mardi Gras Carnival at Apalachicola, Florida. Parades, the selection of an oyster king and queen, and other events held in 1915 continue to be important features of the community's annual seafood festival. Photo courtesy of Florida Photographic Archive

are not duplicated, it is essential to determine what cultural documentation projects, if any, have been previously undertaken within the study area.

Valuable information on maritime heritage can be found in books, articles, census records, wills, deeds, university theses and dissertations, photograph collections, maps, charts, and business records. Helpful publications concerned with natural resources are issued by federal and state agencies such as the U.S. Coast Guard, the National Marine Fisheries Service, and the Sea Grant College extension system. Likely sources of research materials include libraries, historical societies, archives, museums, court houses, newspaper files, and private collections. A number of major publications

devoted to maritime heritage are listed in the bibliography. Two especially useful sources of information: *Directory of Maritime Heritage Resources,* published by the National Trust for Historic Preservation, and *Maritime Folklife Resources,* published by the American Folklife Center at the Library of Congress.[3]

For most research projects, it is important to acquire knowledge about the study area's natural environment, including its climate, seasonal weather patterns, topography, flora, and fauna. If, for example, local fishing traditions are to be investigated, it is essential to know what species are found in local waters and the life cycle of each. Information about the biology of fish and shellfish provides a key to understanding the patterns of behavior of the fishermen who pursue them.

Similarly, it is essential to learn about the laws that regulate commercial and recreational fishing within the study area. Are there different categories of fishing licenses? Is there a "limited entry" system for licensing? Are there specific open and closed fishing seasons? Are there species-specific fishing zones? Do regulations restrict fishing activities to certain types of vessels or gear?

In addition to amassing specific types of information about the environment and laws that regulate its use, researchers should attempt to synthesize data and formulate a history of the relationship between the environment and people. How has the environment shaped human activities? How have human activities altered the environment? What are the principal "seasonal rounds" of activities followed by people within the study area, and how have they changed over time? In order to develop a study area's environmental history, researchers may find it helpful to consult with biologists, ecologists, geographers, soil scientists, and others who are familiar with the region.

Before commencing fieldwork, a researcher should use maps and charts to become more familiar with the study area. Ordinary road maps provide some information about the landscape, but U.S. Geological Service topographical maps and National Oceanic and Atmospheric Administration nautical charts provide much more. Other cartographic aids include maps used by local governments for zoning and property assessment, and maps used by historic preservation organizations to show the locations of sites and properties. Aerial photographs, sometimes obtainable from state departments of natural resources or the offices of county property appraisers, can serve the same function. All these materials can illuminate settlement patterns and locate man-made structures, waterways, landmarks, and fishing grounds. After fieldwork has begun, researchers can draw their own maps or modify existing maps in order to plot features of the landscape such as the distribution of house types, the boundaries of fishing territories, and the locations of significant buildings and navigation landmarks.

Another valuable preliminary activity is a reconnaissance field trip. This is especially useful if researchers are not familiar with the study area. Essentially, the purpose of such a trip is to survey the study area to determine a region's general layout, and to identify features that merit documentation.

The next task is to create a list of potential interviewees. This is done by talking with residents of the study area. Individuals likely to have especially broad views of local maritime activities include harbor masters, fisheries extension agents, fish buyers, and the employees of marine supply stores and bait and tackle shops. Postal clerks, clergymen, town officials, shop keepers, and newspaper reporters may also be good sources of information. When asking questions, researchers should make it clear who they are, what information is being sought, and why the information is being sought. There is no substitute for honesty in such matters. Fieldworkers—especially if they are strangers—may encounter some measure of suspicion on the part of people they contact. While attitudes vary considerably from place to place, it is important to bear in mind that

Crew members of a Seattle fishing boat arrange a seine net on the stern deck as it comes off a power block. Photo by Carl Fleischhauer

inquisitive outsiders are not always viewed in a positive light. Often such attitudes are the result of actual or perceived ill-treatment from marine patrol officers, biologists, and other representatives of state regulatory agencies, as well as agents of the Internal Revenue Service and various types of researchers. A tactic that sometimes helps to acquaint people with research efforts is to submit a news release about the project to the local newspaper. If the release includes a request for assistance, accompanied by the address and telephone number of the project coordinator, area residents may provide suggestions about knowledgeable people to interview and other sources of information. The "Informant Information" form included as Appendix A.1 can be used to develop a file of potential informants.

After a list of potential informants has been drawn up, use it to plan a schedule for interviewing and other types of documentation. For example, if researchers have little understanding of the history of the study area, they might first interview a retired school teacher whom area residents have named as the person most knowledgeable about local history. Similarly, if the project is concerned only with local boat-building traditions, researchers might draw up a list of all local builders, collect basic information about each one, then decide to contact the most experienced builder before speaking with the others. For the purposes of some projects, such as comprehensive surveys of local maritime traditions, it is important to select a representative sample of local residents.

Researchers should be flexible in their work and be prepared to modify their field

23

plan if new leads develop or new sources of information are discovered. If the project is a group effort, regular meetings with other fieldworkers will be needed to share information and to assess the need for any modifications in the work plan. As more and more data are collected, fieldworkers may recognize the need to add or delete certain queries, potential informants, and topics. In addition, experiences in the field may indicate the need to alter documentation techniques.

Before interviewing begins, attempt to determine local standards for meeting a new person. Is it considered appropriate to make initial contact over the telephone? Is an unannounced visit to a person's home by a stranger acceptable? Would an introduction by another resident be the best approach? It is also prudent to learn local views about proper attire, times of the day to visit, and forms of address.

It is often beneficial to use the first face-to-face contact with a potential informant to introduce oneself, explain the project, and obtain more information about the person before getting down to the business of scheduling an interview. It may turn out that the person knows nothing whatsoever about project topics; consequently, it may not be necessary to bring up the subject of an interview. If the person does possess relevant knowledge, the initial meeting can also serve as an opportunity to gather information for use in preparing for the formal interview. On occasion, when the subject is willing and the interviewer is prepared, the initial meeting may also prove to be an appropriate time to conduct an interview. In order to be ready to take advantage of such opportunities, fieldworkers should

have the necessary equipment—tape recorder, tape, notebook, pen or pencil—close at hand (in the car, for example) and ready for immediate use.

To promote successful fieldwork and encourage community support and cooperation, fieldworkers should: (1) be open and honest about the nature of their work; (2) demonstrate enthusiasm for their work; (3) cultivate the skill of listening to what people have to say; (4) be sensitive to appropriate behavior and etiquette; (5) protect sensitive or confidential information elicited from informants; and (6) show informants that their assistance is genuinely appreciated.

Recording observations and other data in a field notebook is an essential fieldwork task. Here fieldworker Nancy Nusz jots fieldnotes while aboard an oyster skiff on Apalachicola Bay, Florida. Photo by David A. Taylor. Courtesy of Bureau of Florida Folklife Programs

Fieldnotes

Every researcher should maintain a field notebook. Fieldnotes are a record of the researcher's activities in the field and should be written up before the end of every day. They should include such things as general observations about the progress of fieldwork, impressions of persons who have been interviewed, summaries of conversations, descriptions of settings, and drawings and diagrams of buildings and other artifacts. They should also include information that is useful for the interpretation of project documents, such as lighting conditions during photography and sources of extraneous sounds picked up by a tape recorder.[4] Maintaining a field notebook or fieldnote files in a portable computer is an excellent way of preserving small bits of data that may seem insignificant at the time of entry but will take on importance after fieldwork is completed. At the very least, fieldnotes provide a useful chronology of the fieldworker's activities. At best, they are the intellectual core of a project's documentation, preserving the observations and ruminations of the fieldworker as the project unfolds.

Interviewing

Interviewing is an efficient technique for gathering data and the one most often used by many cultural specialists. When a fieldworker conducts an interview, he or she must determine the amount of control to be applied. A nondirected interview encourages discussion of a wide range of topics that are largely determined by the interests of the informant. A directed interview is usually characterized by the interviewer's attention to very specific topics and questions. Sometimes the interviewer may change the approach. For example, an interviewer might switch from a directed to a nondirected approach if it becomes evident that an informant's storehouse of traditional knowledge presents an unusual opportunity for the documentation of many general aspects of local culture. Data elicited during interviews can be recorded in writing in the form of fieldnotes, or as answers to questions on a questionnaire. They can also be recorded verbatim on audio tape with a tape recorder, or recorded both aurally and visually on videotape with a video camera and sound unit. In the case of interviews recorded on audio or video tape, it is proper to ask the informant to sign a consent form in order to establish that he or she has given permission for the use of information on the tape. The text of the form should specify as accurately as possible where the tape recording will be deposited and how it may be used. If the informant wishes to place restrictions on the use of the recording, these restrictions should be written on the form. A sample "Informant Consent" form is included as Appendix A.2.

There is no question that tape-recorded interviews are an effective way to collect information. To those unfamiliar with fieldwork, interviewing on tape may appear to be the easiest task imaginable: just turn on the tape recorder and let the person talk. But to obtain maximum value, a tape-recorded interview should not be viewed as a replacement for background research or as a substitute for taking notes. Furthermore, since one's time in the field is limited, it is necessary to prepare thoroughly for interviews. Learn as much as possible about the topic or topics to be discussed. Attempt to anticipate the kind of expertise

the informant possesses before the interview. Jot down notes in advance concerning topics to be explored. A novice should practice interviewing with a fellow team member, friend, or family member before entering the field. The experience of being interviewed is equally instructive and contributes to a keen appreciation of the process.

Interviews recorded on tape are documents that not only benefit the collector, but, if preserved in a repository such as a library, museum, or archive, can also assist future researchers. The interviewer should bear in mind that others not present at the time of the actual interview may someday listen to the tape. To facilitate full and proper comprehension of the interview, pay close attention to the technical quality of the recording, and try to clarify all issues discussed. If, for example, an informant says, "I caught a fish this big," and holds his or her hands apart to indicate the size, the interviewer should say, "Oh, about thirty inches" (or whatever length is appropriate), in order to clarify the approximate size for the benefit of those who listen to the recording later on.

Since the field recording should represent, as accurately as possible, the communicative event involving the interviewer and the subject, the interviewer should not turn the recorder on and off during the interview in an effort to save tape. Moreover, if the interviewer frequently turns the recorder on and off when the subject is speaking, the subject can easily form the impression that the interviewer considers some statements to be less valuable than

others. Fieldworkers should bring an adequate supply of tape and be prepared to let the recorder run as freely as possible.

The use of tape catalog forms, to be filled out by the collector as soon as possible after each interview, is essential. Completed catalog forms strengthen the value of recordings by providing detailed outlines of their contents. Even if full, verbatim transcriptions of field recordings are to be made later on—often an expensive and time-consuming process—the preparation of catalogs is still beneficial. An "Audio Tape Log" form is included as Appendix A.3.

Interviewing is a skill of some complexity. Available guides to the subject include Edward D. Ives's *The Tape-Recorded Interview: A Guide for Fieldworkers in Folklore and Oral History,* Bruce Jackson's *Fieldwork,* and Kenneth S. Goldstein's *A Guide for Field Workers in Folklore.*[5] These works cover such key topics as selecting informants, learning to use recording equipment, keeping fieldnotes, using interviewing strategies, and cataloging and transcribing field tapes. These topics are also covered in the instructional videotape program on interviewing, *An Oral Historians Work,* that features explanations and demonstrations by seasoned interviewer Edward D. Ives.[6]

Sound Recordings

A researcher's level of craftsmanship with tape-recorded interviews is evidenced not only by interviewing skill, but by the ability to produce recordings of high quality. The achievement of high-quality sound recordings relates to the type of recorder, microphone, and tape used, the way the equipment is set up, and the choice of recording site.

Bernard Miller of Eastpoint, Florida, tosses a cast net. Photo by David A. Taylor (FMP86–BDT015/27)

27

Shrimp fisherman Charles Herrin of Jacksonville, Florida, explains an aspect of the design of his boat during a tape-recorded interview conducted in his home by field-worker David Taylor. Photo by LeeEllen Friedland (FMP87–BLF004/10)

Audiocassette tape recorders, if carefully used, can give very satisfactory results. By and large, more expensive models ($200 to $500) offer the best performance, but good results can be obtained with less-expensive machines. Although the size of the very smallest recorders may be attractive, researchers should consider that slightly larger machines often provide some of the following desirable features: the use of larger batteries and hence greater battery capacity; an easy-to-read volume (VU) meter that indicates the recording level (and often the condition of the batteries as well); a line- or auxiliary-level input to permit the copying of other recordings, the recording of an event directly from a public address system, or the like; and, occasionally, the ability to choose between automatic and manual control of recording levels. The very best recordings are made with professional open-reel equipment. In the near future, this equipment will likely be surpassed by a new generation of portable digital recorders.

If interviews are structured so that the informant does most of the talking, a monaural recorder will probably suffice.

Even with the use of a clip-on microphone an interviewer's questions will be heard, although with an "off-mike" quality. On the other hand, if the interviews are structured as dialogue or if interviews are conducted with two or more individuals, a stereo recorder and two microphones may well be called for. A stereo recorder may also be useful for recording events or activities other than interviews. A professional sound recordist, however, may be needed to make a high-quality recording of, say, a church service or the verbal exchanges between workers on the deck of a fishing vessel. And certain types of musical performance may best be recorded in a studio.

Regardless of the type of recorder, the two most important factors in producing a good recording are the placement of the microphone and the control of ambient sound. External cardioid, lavaliere, or clip-on microphones are recommended over internal, built-in microphones that pick up excessive amounts of machine noise and ambient sounds. Because ambient noise increases in proportion to the distance between the microphone and the subject, it is important to place the microphone as close as possible to the subject's mouth. A cardioid microphone can be attached to a boom and suspended above and in front of the subject's head. A lavaliere or clip-on microphone can be easily fastened to the subject's clothing.

The type of recording tape used is an important consideration. For best results, use high-quality, name-brand tape. Researchers who use cassette tapes usually select sixty-minute cassettes (thirty minutes per side). Longer tapes—those over forty-five minutes per side—are thinner and more susceptible to stretching or breaking. Cassettes held together with screws are better than those held together with glue because they can be easily disassembled for repair of broken or jammed tape. Researchers who employ open-reel machines usually prefer tape with a thickness of 1.5 mils because tape of this thickness is stronger and subject to less "print through" than thinner tape.

The recording site is another important factor in achieving high-quality recordings. Since field interviews are usually conducted in a subject's home or work place rather than in a sound studio, the researcher must select a location within such areas offering the best possibility for a clear recording. This might mean choosing a room with carpets and curtains, which minimize the reverberation of sound, or selecting the room furthest from a noisy street. If a television or radio is playing, or a fan is whirling, the researcher might request that they be turned off during the interview. Although fieldworkers may feel hesitant about these requests, those "who work carefully with good equipment convey to the informant how much they value his words and thus produce a flattering and positive effect."[7]

In order to facilitate the preservation of a field recording, copies should be made as soon as possible and used for cataloging and transcribing so the original tape can be spared the wear and tear. In short, the original recording should be viewed as the "master" and protected accordingly.

Participant-Observation

One of the best ways to understand the forms and functions of maritime traditions is to take part in the day-to-day activities of the community. The premise underlying participant-observation, as this approach is called, is that the researcher becomes a more effective observer by taking an active role in the performance of regular activities—by assisting a local cook with the preparation of seafood gumbo, for example, or by working as a deckhand on a shrimp boat. The approach also demonstrates to members of the community the researcher's commitment to the documentation of maritime heritage. In many cases, involvement with such ordinary chores as

cleaning fish, culling oysters, or shoveling ice into a hold will not only enhance the researcher's understanding of the processes, techniques, and words associated with these activities, but will also result in better rapport with informants.

How does one arrange to be a participant observer in a maritime community? Usually, it is best not to broach the subject too early in a relationship. Once rapport has been established, many community members will spontaneously issue an invitation: "Well, if you really want to learn about oystering, the

Fieldworker Gerald Parsons of the American Folklife Center (right) participates in railbird hunting on the Maurice River near Port Elizabeth, New Jersey. Parsons's participant-observation was conducted in 1984 in conjunction with the center's Pinelands Folklife Project. Photo by Dennis McDonald (84BDM235042–08–35)

Shrimper Charles Herrin empties shrimp and other marine creatures onto the deck of his trawler. Understanding how a task such as this fits into the sequence of activities that occurs during the course of a fishing trip is an important task for the field-worker. Photo by David A. Taylor (FMP86–BDT001/34)

In some cases, it may not be possible both to observe and to participate. This is especially likely with activities that require a high level of expertise or are conducted at a pace required to meet a production schedule. For example, professional boat builders are seldom interested in taking the time required to teach their multiple skills to a novice because they usually cannot afford to interrupt their work schedules. Consequently, unless the researcher already possesses the skills necessary to be hired by a boat builder, or can place an order for a boat and convince the builder that he or she should be permitted to help build it, probably the best one can hope for is to be allowed to observe boatbuilding activities and, when time permits, to interview the builder. There are, however, a number of activities common to maritime communities that the researcher can try without a great deal of difficulty. These include tasks that are basically simple and repetitive, such as cooking, mending nets, sorting fish, filling bait bags, and poling a boat.

Although it is sometimes necessary to formally request permission to be a participant-observer, as in the case of filleting fish at a fish plant, in most instances opportunities to try one's hand at an activity arise naturally. The researcher who has gone along on a fishing trip mainly to observe activities and take photographs may, for example, see a chance to help the crew sort fish. Researchers should always be on the lookout for such opportunities. However, one should never be pushy about participating: wait for a direct offer or obtain permission first.

Inshore fishing activities are among those best suited for participant-observation.

best way would be for you to come out in the boat with me." Others, many of whom assume that "everyone knows about these things," will have to be convinced that inviting the researcher to observe and participate in their work is a good idea. As with all initial contacts, the researcher should provide a clear explanation of why he or she is conducting research, what topics are being investigated, how information is being collected, and what will be done with the collected data.

31

After obtaining permission from an experienced fisherman to go along on a fishing trip, it is important to determine the time of departure, destination, and approximate time of return. The researcher should find out what personal gear and supplies should be obtained, including special clothing such as gloves, rubber boots, and foulweather gear; a life preserver; tools; and food. Since in some areas all persons engaged in commercial fishing must be properly licensed, ask whether a license or permission from an official is required. Before the trip, it is also a good idea to go aboard the boat and check out the arrangement of space and the availability of running water, cooking equipment, and restroom facilities. Since boats, especially small inshore craft, are sometimes not outfitted with "heads" (restrooms), this is a detail that many researchers (especially female researchers) will not want to overlook.

In most cases a notebook, pens, pencils, camera, and film are the best equipment for the documentation of fishing. Because these items may be exposed to the elements, it is advisable to keep them in a plastic bag, rucksack, or other waterproof container. Bring along several pens and pencils, plenty of film in a variety of speeds, lens-cleaning fluid and tissue, and a spare battery for the camera. Also bring along a couple of rubber bands to keep the pages of the field notebook from blowing around if the wind comes up. Tape recording interviews on a boat may be hindered by the noise created by the vessel's engines.[8] Furthermore, it may not be possible for the fishermen to take time from their normal activities to participate in an interview. However, some types of fishing trips, especially those which are characterized by long periods of slack time, can be conducive to tape recording. The feasibility of making sound recordings should be determined before the trip. If the decision is made to bring recording equipment, be sure to carry along enough fresh batteries.

Before leaving on the fishing trip, write down a list of topics to be investigated on board the boat. These might include:

- names and uses of boat spaces and gear
- sequence of fishing operations
- information needed to locate fishing areas
- roles of crewmen
- ages and working experience of crewmen
- family ties between crewmen
- names fishermen use for birds, fish, landmarks, and fishing grounds
- approximate times of fishing operations, rest periods, and meals
- jokes, stories, and other narratives
- beliefs
- customs
- communication with fishermen on other boats
- navigation techniques, including the use of landmarks

While aboard a fishing boat, researchers should be honest about the amount of experience they have had with fishing. There is no point in pretending to be experienced. In fact, if the researcher is recognized as a novice, fishermen will often go out of their way to explain the basic details—the how and the why—of their activities; such details would not be articulated under normal circumstances. Moreover, because fishing can be hazardous, even for the most experienced fisherman, be sure to ask the crewmen to identify the safest places to stand during fishing operations. Although fishermen will probably be content to let the researcher stand back and observe their work, write notes, and take photographs, it is worthwhile to volunteer to help with some aspect of the work. If the offer is accepted, assistance will lighten fishermen's work load, and also give them cause to view the researcher as a "good sport" and a person "not too proud to get his hands dirty."

In order to understand the meaning of the activities taking place on the boat, "begin very generally and let the patterns of movement, smells, noises and colors *suggest their own structure* to you.[9] Throughout the fishing trip try to determine the flow of work. How are decisions reached about when and where to fish? What is the regular sequence of activities involved with setting and retrieving gear? What are the specific responsibilities of each crewman? How is information communicated between crewmen? When do periods of intense activity occur? When are the slack times? Because most types of fishing involve the repetition of a particular sequence of actions, it is likely that the researcher will have several opportunities to observe the performance of the "core technique" characteristic of the fishery.

If time permits, it is instructive to make more than one trip on the same boat in

Fieldworker Nancy Nusz uses a 35-mm camera to photograph Apalachicola, Florida, oysterman Cletus Anderson culling his catch. Photo by David A. Taylor (FMP86–BDT025/6)

Photography

order to verify observations made on the first trip. Additional trips can also be made to study how changes in gear, weather, time of year, and depth of water influence fishing.

Photography

Photography is an invaluable tool for recording many subjects of cultural significance, from single artifacts to complicated events. A detailed discussion of the merits of photography as a research tool is beyond the scope of the present publication, but the reader is advised to consult John and Malcolm Collier's *Visual Anthropology: Photography as a Research Tool* and Bruce Jackson's *Fieldwork*.[10]

Today, the standard equipment for still photography in the field is the 35-mm single lens reflex (SLR) camera with interchangeable lenses. Since it is often beneficial to make a photographic record on color as well as on black-and-white film, access to two camera bodies with an identical lens mounting system is desirable. Due to advances made in electronics in recent years, modern 35-mm cameras are relatively easy to operate. Most possess "automatic" modes that require the photographer to do little more than focus and press the shutter release.

The choice of color or black-and-white film should be based on how the photographs will be used. For example, if a publication will be the result of a documentation project, black-and-white film is probably the appropriate choice in most cases. If the main vehicle for communication will be a slide show, then color slides are the better choice. The goals of some projects will dictate that fieldworkers use both color and black-and-white film for documentation. A wide assortment of slow and fast films designed for various lighting conditions are available—slower films for bright light and faster films for low light. In order to obtain the best possible photographs under field conditions, researchers should carry several rolls of film suited to different levels of light. In settings where very low light prevails, the use of an electronic flash (strobe) and/or a sturdy tripod may be advantageous.

When planning how photography will be conducted in the field, it is advisable to draw up a schedule of photographic tasks. Most field photography can be assigned to one of four subject categories: human activities, portraits, artifacts, and photographs in an informant's collection. Each of these presents particular problems for the photographer and calls for the application of certain equipment or techniques.

When photographing human activities, 24-mm and 35-mm wide-angle lenses are useful for capturing two or more people relating to each other, to their work, and to interior space. Complete coverage of human activities requires taking a variety of medium and close-up shots while walking all the way around the scene. In order to ensure that every step of a process is recorded, fieldworkers should learn to take many photographs. Later, copies of photos can be used to great advantage in eliciting detailed information from informants about the various steps in the process—details that might otherwise escape the attention of the fieldworker.

Portrait photography is usually conducted with lenses with focal lengths of 85-mm to 135-mm. When taking portrait photos, tripods may be used to increase camera steadiness. People who pose for portraits are usually more conscious of the pho-

Photographs can be used to effectively convey processes and sequences. These images, selected from several hundred documenting the construction of Charles Herrin's fifty-two-foot shrimp trawler, Miss Joann, *at Mayport, Florida, illustrate key stages of the construction project. (1) Charles Herrin (right) and his brothers, Donald (left) and Thomas, erect a side timber. Photos by David A. Taylor. Courtesy of Bureau of Florida Folklife Programs (2) Deck of* Miss Joann *after tar paper has been laid. (3) Thomas Herrin nails the forward end of a plank in place. (4) Thomas (left) and Charles Herrin install a plank. (5) Thomas Herrin uses a hammer and a putty knife to drive caulking material into plank seams at the stern of the* Miss Joann. *(6) After her launch,* Miss Joann *nears completion at a Mayport dock.*

tographer than are those who are engaged in activities. Frequently subjects will stiffen up and assume an extremely grave demeanor. It is the fieldworker's responsibility to make the subject feel at ease so that a more natural image may be recorded. Usually this can be achieved if good rapport is established. It is often helpful for the photographer to explain the type of shot that he or she would like to take and how the equipment will be used to achieve that end.

With artifact photography, it is important to take photographs of each artifact from a variety of angles in order to record its basic characteristics. With complex objects, take close-up shots of significant features as well. So that viewers of photographs will be able to discern the size of the artifact, it is advisable to place a suitable object of known size—a coin, a ruler, a range pole—next to it for at least one shot. For example, when photographing buildings a range pole marked off in one-foot intervals and a shorter measuring stick marked off in feet and inches are appropriate for most shots. Photographers should pay close attention to background and depth of field to ensure that the artifact is sharply depicted on film. With large, immovable artifacts, such as houses, the photographer should select lighting conditions and viewing angles that depict them to best advantage. Small artifacts can be placed in front of contrasting backgrounds. Because tripods increase camera stability and permit longer exposure times, they are useful for artifact photography.

Fieldworkers are often given permission to copy photographs in private collections. While it is sometimes possible to borrow photographs and take them to a profes-sional photo lab to be copied, if copies are made at the owner's home the chance of losing originals is eliminated.[11] Copies can be made with a 35-mm camera and a standard copy stand consisting of an adjustable camera mount, a platform upon which the photo rests, and bright lights for illuminating the photo. An acceptable substitute can be improvised by inverting the center column of a tripod, affixing the camera to the mount, and using adjustable lamps or natural light to illuminate the subject photo. Special attachments for close-up work, or "micro" or "macro" lenses, are highly recommended for copying photographs and other small objects. When copying photos, fieldworkers should bear in mind that a photo itself is an artifact. In order to convey this, it is important to take at least one shot of the entire photo, including its borders.

Although it is impossible to predict all the photographic problems that may occur in maritime settings, it is possible to note a few that fieldworkers are likely to encounter. When photographing on and around water, glare from reflected sunlight is a frequent annoyance. In order to reduce glare, one may wish to consider attaching a polarizing filter to the camera lens. These filters are relatively inexpensive and may be purchased at most camera shops. Another problem is damage to equipment resulting from contact with water, especially salt water. Photography on moving boats, for example, nearly always exposes photographic gear to spray. To cut down on exposure to water, equipment not in use should be kept in a plastic bag or some other waterproof container. In addition, it is important to change film and lenses in protected areas to ensure that water does not enter a camera's internal mechanisms. If underwater photography is required, special waterproof housings and waterproof cameras can be obtained at a variety of prices. One other problem that often confronts fieldworkers is achieving good photographic coverage in confined spaces, such as boat cabins and small workshops. This problem is easily solved with the use of wide-angle lenses. In such situations, 24–mm and 28–mm lenses are especially useful.

In order to permit proper cataloging and analysis, it is necessary to record all pertinent data about each photograph. General information about the photo session (such as date, place, names of subjects, description of scene, and name of photographer) should be recorded in the fieldnotes at the end of each day of photography. The cataloging of individual images will probably not occur until after the film has been processed and converted into slides or negatives. After processing, data pertinent to each image can be entered on a form, such as the "Photograph Log" included as Appendix A.4. Black-and-white films can be more efficiently cataloged and filed if a contact sheet is made of each roll. The filing of slides is enhanced with the use of archival-quality slide storage sheets.

If a project's fieldworkers are not experienced photographers, or if the production of high-quality photographs is important for the success of a project, it may be a good idea to obtain the services of a professional photographer.

Documenting Artifacts

The investigation of many topics is required for a full understanding of any item of culture within its natural setting. Documentation of items of material culture should begin with a review of published and unpublished information pertaining to the type of artifact to be documented. Although the nature of information sought will vary according to the goals of the project and the expertise of researchers, central topics to be investigated include distribution, design, construction, and use. Moving from the general class of artifacts to the specific example to be documented in the field, researchers should ascertain:

- the date of its creation
- the name of its designer
- the name of its maker
- the names of present and past owners
- its uses
- the materials of which it is made
- its component parts
- modifications to its structure or use
- its significance to the community

The next step in the documentation process is the recording of physical properties. This can be accomplished through the application of techniques such as photography, drawings, field observation, and measurement of principal dimensions. Because boats and buildings are two of the most prominent types of artifacts to be found in maritime communities, additional comments about the documentation of their physical properties are in order.

Boats are an important and conspicuous class of objects in maritime culture, and they often exhibit regional differences in form, construction, and use as a result of adaptation to specific environmental conditions and use requirements. For example, the light "glades skiff" is well suited to the calm, shallow waters of the everglades of south Florida. Other types, such as the Maine lobster boat, the New Jersey sneakbox, the Lake Superior fish tug, and the Louisiana pirogue, possess forms that have evolved as builders attempted to improve their suitability to local contexts. Because of their importance to residents of maritime communities, boats are prime candidates for documentation.

In many cases, the documentation of the forms of boats requires specialized skills and knowledge. It is especially important to learn how to take accurate measurements by hand. Unlike buildings and other artifacts that possess straight lines and flat surfaces, boats often have complicated shapes based on complex curves. Such shapes, which generally vary greatly over the length of a hull, make the accurate recording of hull forms a painstaking and time-consuming task and call for the use of certain tools and techniques. In addition, to ensure that component parts of vessels are properly identified, it is necessary to become familiar with standard terminology as well as localized terms. An excellent reference work for standard terminology is René de Kerchove's *International Maritime Dictionary*.[12]

If the goal of a project is to document local craft so that exact forms can be preserved, then the desired end product of fieldwork is probably a set of accurate lines plans and a table of offsets for each boat. In addition to preserving boat forms graphically, such data can be used to build replicas and to study local design and construction practices. If the project requires the pro-

duction of high-quality lines plans, it may be necessary to hire a naval architect to record the hull form and execute drawings. Alternatively, researchers may elect to learn how to "take the lines" of a vessel and supply these data to a naval architect or competent draftsman for conversion to a lines plan. For projects that do not demand professional-quality lines plans, it may be possible for fieldworkers to record hull measurements and execute adequate lines plans for small craft (under twenty feet). Essentially, "taking the lines" is a process of obtaining measurements from an existing hull, recording these measurements in a standard table of offsets, and then using these measurements to draft (or loft) in two dimensions the set of drawings that defines the hull form. The amount of time required to learn this process will vary, but it is probably safe to say that a person can acquire the basic skills necessary for small craft documentation in a week or less.

The best way to learn is to observe an experienced person take the lines of a boat, then imitate the lines taker's actions. If such an opportunity is not available, one may learn the basics by studying published descriptions of the process, then practicing with an actual boat, preferably a boat under twenty feet in length. Fieldworkers must bear in mind that no single methodology can be used for the documentation of all vessels. Lines-taking techniques must be modified in accordance with such factors as vessel size, shape, and location. Techniques are discussed by John Gardner in his articles "Taking Lines Off Bigger Boats," "Taking Off Lines Allows Duplication of Existing Boats," and "Triangulation Method is Well Suited to Lifting Lines"; by Walter J. Sim-

mons in his book *Lines, Lofting and Half Models;* and by David A. Taylor in his article "Taking the Lines."[13] The lofting procedure is clearly explained in Allan H. Vaitses's book *Lofting.*[14] A concise description of how the lines of a particular small boat were taken off in the field is given in Appendix B.2 of this book. If the project's goal is merely to record the general characteristics of local boats, then fieldworkers can record key measurements and other significant details. A boat documentation form that can be used for the latter purpose is included as Appendix A.5.

For a thorough documentation of a vessel, it is necessary to gather a variety of contextual data. These data include information about the history of boat building and boat use in the area, as well as information about the designer, builder, owner, and the uses of, and modifications to, each boat to be documented.

Properly executed measured drawings are the most accurate record of a building. Unfortunately, exact scale drawings can be expensive to produce since they often require the services of an architect or draftsman. However, for the purposes of many projects, serviceable drawings can be produced by fieldworkers who do not possess formal training in architecture.

Before measurement activities commence, it is important to decide which buildings should be measured, how much time and personnel can be devoted to the task, and the manner in which the work should be conducted. Since it is essential to understand the structure of a building in order to determine what types of drawings should be made, it is beneficial to make a preliminary survey. Because it is seldom

Photos and other items collected by informants are valuable sources of information about life in maritime communities. This page from the scrapbook of Alex Kellam of Crisfield, Maryland, includes a photo, a poem, and captions written by Kellam. Photo by Carl Fleischhauer (AFC 45/28)

possible to record every detail of a building, the fieldworker must decide what features of the structure to record and the types of drawings and their complexity. As Harley J. McKee points out in *Recording Historic Buildings: The Historic American Building Survey,* several types of drawings can be made, including location plan (which locates the property with reference to highways, towns, and natural features), plot plan (which indicates the building's relationship to structures, gardens, or other features of the immediate environment), floor plan (which records room layout, and locations of doors, windows, stairways, and structural supports of each level of the building), and exterior elevation (which represents the facade of a building projected on a vertical plane).[15]

With regard to the measurement of the actual structure, best results are obtained by recording measurements by hand. This can be efficiently accomplished by three-person teams; two to take measurements and one to record measurements in a field notebook. Two can accurately collect data if one calls out measurements and the other records them. Because it is difficult to measure large surfaces without assistance, single fieldworkers cannot work as efficiently. To ensure that field measurements are properly interpreted when it is time to use them to produce a scale drawing, it is helpful to sketch the feature to be measured in the field notebook before measuring begins. Then, as measurements are taken, they can be written alongside corresponding aspects of the sketch. Measuring devices employed by fieldworkers include steel tapes, folding rules, and straight rules. A profile gauge can be used to record the shapes of moulding.

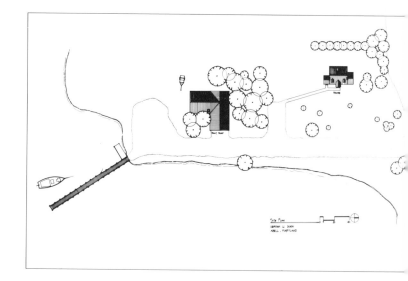

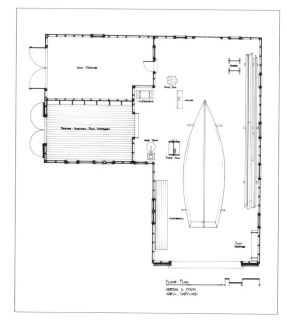

Floor plan of Herman W. Dixon's boatshop showing arrangement of workspace, tools, materials, and boat. Plan by William J. Bonstra and William D. McGowan. Plan courtesy of Calvert Marine Museum

Site plan of property of boat builder Herman W. Dixon of Abell, Maryland. This plan was executed in 1983 by architecture students William J. Bonstra and William D. McGowan for the Calvert Marine Museum, Solomons, Maryland. Their work was part of an exhibit project, funded by the National Endowment for the Arts, Folk Arts Program, that resulted in the museum's permanent exhibit, "Built to Work: Building Deadrise Workboats in Southern Maryland." Plan courtesy of Calvert Marine Museum

In addition to other data noted above, measurements of buildings should be supplemented by interior and exterior photographs, and by inventories of furnishings and sketches of their placement. Artifacts found within the structure or on its property are particularly significant, and they should be fully documented. A sample building documentation form, which can be used to record measurements and other data, is included as Appendix A.6.

After You Leave the Field

Upon the completion of fieldwork, researchers should move on to the business of cataloging and analyzing the data that has been collected. This work, some of which should have already been accomplished in the field, includes such tasks as cataloging tape recordings and photographic materials, and evaluating the body of field data. If analysis reveals that some critical item of information was not collected, it may be necessary to return to the field to obtain it.

Another post-fieldwork activity is the preparation of field data for a repository. This includes proper identification, cataloging, and packaging of all materials in accordance with the repository's standard procedures. If duplicate copies of tape recordings or other materials are required by project researchers, it may be advantageous to make them before the originals are placed in a repository, since some repositories may not be equipped to handle this chore after the materials have been turned over. It is important to work closely with repository personnel to ensure that materials are prepared in a manner most conducive to preservation and full use by other researchers.

Fieldworkers should express their appreciation to individuals who have assisted with the project. Face-to-face expressions of gratitude are appropriate, as are thank-you letters on letterhead stationery when the project has been sponsored by an institution. If photography and sound recording have been important parts of documentation efforts, copies of photographs and taped interviews make suitable gifts for people who have been helpful. If a publication, exhibit, or film results from the project, acknowledge the assistance of local residents in print. The way that fieldworkers express their gratitude will likely influence the level of cooperation accorded any future researchers.

It is always a sound practice to keep people in the study area informed about the project. In particular, those from whom information has been collected should be kept abreast of plans for the use of the materials. If some product will result—article, book, or exhibit—find ways to share it with them.

Ethics

Ethics play a critical role in field research. Researchers must be truthful about the purpose of their inquiries and should ensure that information elicited from people does not cause them harm. Commitments given about maintaining the anonymity of informants or the confidentiality of information should always be honored. Researchers should be sensitive to the fact that many issues can be divisive within a community and that revealing certain kinds of information may have serious implications. For example, divulging information about a man's fishing territories or about the code words he uses over the CB radio to let a kinsman know he has located a school of fish could interfere with his ability to earn an income. Although informants often reveal a great deal of private knowledge to the researcher, the researcher should not assume that this information is for public dissemination. Occasionally, the researcher will face the dilemma of choosing between accurately communicating the information that he or she has collected and the responsibility to the people from whom information has been acquired. Since there are no general guidelines that will resolve this dilemma in all cases, the researcher will have to rely on his or her sense of justice and honesty.[16]

---

[1] A good procedural outline for project planning can be found in Anne Derry et al., *Guidelines for Local Surveys: A Guide for Preservation Planning*, National Register Bulletin 24, rev. ed. (Washington: National Register of Historic Places, Interagency Resources Division, U.S. Department of the Interior, 1985), 9–27.

[2] See, for example, The Foundation Center, *The Foundation Directory*, 13th ed. (New York: The Foundation Center, 1991); and David G. Bauer, *The "How To" Grants Manual: Successful Grantseeking Techniques for Obtaining Public and Private Grants* (New York: American Council on Education; Macmillan, 1988).

[3] National Trust for Historic Preservation, *Directory of Maritime Heritage Resources* (Washington: National Trust for Historic Preservation, 1984); Peter Bartis and Mary Hufford, *Maritime Folklife Resources: A Directory and Index*, Publications of the American Folklife Center, no. 5 (Washington: Library of Congress, 1980).

[4] Fieldworkers should ensure the confidentiality of fieldnotes that relate to highly sensitive information provided by informants, and notes which contain the fieldworker's candid observations about individuals in the study area. One technique is to record confidential information in a log separate from the main fieldnotes.

[5] Edward D. Ives, *The Tape-Recorded Interview: A Manual for Field Workers in Folklore and Oral History* (Knoxville: University of Tennessee Press, 1980); Bruce Jackson, *Fieldwork* (Urbana and Chicago: University of Illinois Press, 1987); Kenneth S. Goldstein, *A Guide for Field Workers in Folklore* (Hatboro, Pa.: Folklore Associates, 1964).

[6] Northeast Archives of Folklore and Oral History, *An Oral Historian's Work, with Dr. Edward Ives*. 30-minute color videotape (Orono, Me.: Northeast Archives of Folklore and Oral History, 1987).

[7] Carl Fleischhauer, "Sound Recording and Still Photography in the Field," in *Handbook of American Folklore*, edited by Richard M. Dorson (Bloomington: Indiana University Press, 1986), 384–90.

[8] Of course, in order to achieve the goals of some projects, it may be desirable to tape record the sounds of engines, deck machinery, marine radios, waves, and other ambient noise.

[9] Robert H. Byington, "Strategies for Collecting Occupational Folklife in Contemporary Urban/Industrial Contexts," in *Working Americans: Contemporary Approaches to Occupational Folklife*, Robert H. Byington, ed., Smithsonian Folklife Studies, no. 3 (Los Angeles: California Folklore Society, 1978), 51.

[10] John Collier, Jr., and Malcolm Collier, *Visual Anthropology: Photography as a Research Tool*, rev. and expanded ed. (Albuquerque: University of New Mexico Press, 1986); Bruce Jackson, *Fieldwork*, 194–256.

[11] However, if it is desirable to borrow photographs (or other artifacts) from private collections, the use of an artifact loan form, such as the one included as Appendix A.7, is recommended.

[12] René de Kerchove, *International Maritime Dictionary: An Encyclopedic Dictionary of Useful Maritime Terms with Equivalents in French and German*, 2nd rev. ed. (New York: Van Nostrand Reinhold, 1983).

[13] John Gardner, "Taking Lines Off Bigger Boats," *National Fisherman* 67, no. 1 (May 1986), 58, "Taking Off Lines Allows Duplication of Existing Boats," *National Fisherman* 66, no. 12 (April 1986): 44–45, and "Triangulation Method is Well Suited to Lifting Lines," *National Fisherman* 67, no. 4 (August 1986): 65–67; Walter J. Simmons, *Lines, Lofting and Half Models* (Lincolnville, Me.: Ducktrap Woodworking, 1991); and David Taylor, "Taking the Lines," *Woodenboat* 19 (Nov.-Dec. 1977): 42–45. A detailed set of standards for the documentation of vessels, similar in rigor to McKee's *Recording Historic Buildings*, can be found in Richard K. Anderson's *Guidelines for Recording Historic Ships* (Washington: National Park Service, U.S. Department of the Interior, Historic American Engineering Record,

1988). Several techniques for taking the lines of small boats are presented in Paul Lipke, ed., *Boats: A Field Manual for the Documentation of Small Craft* (Nashville: American Association for State and Local History, forthcoming).

¹⁴ Allan H. Vaitses, *Lofting* (Camden, Me.: International Marine Publishing Co., 1980).

¹⁵ Harley J. McKee, *Recording Historic Buildings: The Historic American Buildings Survey* (Washington: U. S. Department of the Interior, National Park Service, 1970), 24–25.

¹⁶ For a detailed statement on professional ethics, see: American Anthropological Association, *Professional Ethics: Statements and Procedures of the American Anthropological Association* (Washington: American Anthropological Association, 1983).

Native Americans fishing for salmon at Celilo Falls, Columbia River, Oregon, in September, 1941. Photo by Russell Lee. Courtesy of Prints and Photographs Division, Library of Congress (LC-USF 34–70154-D)

Appendixes

INFORMANT INFORMATION

Fieldworker: _____ Project: _____

Date: _____

Name: (Last) _____ (First) _____ (Middle) _____

Address _____

City: _____ State: _____ Zip: _____

Phone: ( ) _____

Birth Date: _____ Place: _____

Occupation: _____ Ethnicity: _____

Special knowledge or skill: _____

Comments: _____

_Jeff Broussard (left)
and Bill Holland
working on a tradi-
tional Biloxi lugger
hull at Holland's
boatyard in Biloxi,
Mississippi. Photo
by Tom Rankin_

INFORMANT CONSENT FORM

Thank you for participating in the _____ Project. By signing the form below, you give your permission to include any tapes and/or photographs made during the _____ Project in a public archive, where they will be available to researchers and the public for scholarly and educational purposes. By giving your permission, you do not give up any copyright or performance rights you may hold.

I agree to the uses of these materials described above, except for any restrictions listed below.

_____
(signature)

_____
(date)

_____
(researcher signature)

Restrictions:

AUDIO TAPE LOG

ITEM NUMBER: _____ PROJECT: _____

FIELDWORKER(S): _____

INFORMANT(S): _____

DATE & PLACE OF RECORDING: _____

RECORDING EQUIPMENT USED: _____

TAPE FORMAT: _____ REEL-TO-REEL _____ CASSETTE

TAPE SIZE (e.g., 7 in. reel, 60 cassette, etc.): _____

RECORDING CONFIGURATION: _____ stereo machine, recorded in stereo

_____ stereo machine, recorded in mono

_____ mono machine

Counter No.	Tape Contents

Appendix:

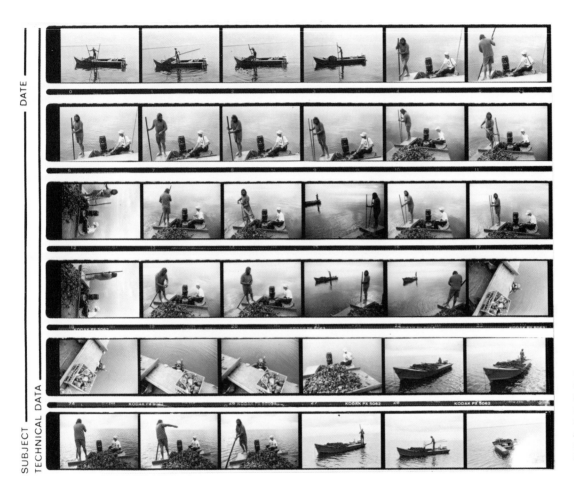

Contact sheet with images depicting activities of oystermen Ken Folsom and Cletus Anderson described in fieldnotes. Photos by David A. Taylor (FMP86–BDT026)

PHOTOGRAPH LOG

ITEM NUMBER: PROJECT:

FIELDWORKER(S):

SUBJECT(S)/EVENT(S):

DATE(S) & PLACE(S) OF PHOTOS:

FILM TYPE: CAMERA:

Neg. or Slide No.	Description

BOAT DOCUMENTATION FORM

Fieldworker:

Project:

Date:

1. Name of vessel:

2. Basic vessel type and local name of type:

3. Vessel registration number:

4. Location of vessel:

5. Name and address of present owner:

6. Name and address of present user:

7. Present use of vessel:

8. Significance of vessel (rare vessel type, outstanding example of type, work of important designer or builder, significance to community, connection to important people or events):

PHYSICAL HISTORY

9. Date and place of construction:

10. Names and addresses of designer and builder:

_____

_____

11. Names of previous owners and dates of ownership:

_____

_____

_____

12. Previous uses of vessel:

_____

_____

_____

_____

13. Description (with dates) of known alterations and additions:

_____

_____

_____

_____

_____

PHYSICAL DESCRIPTION

Principal Dimensions

14. Length overall (LOA):

15. Waterline length (LWL):

16. Maximum breadth (beam):

17. Depth:

18. Draft:

19. Hull type (round-bottom, flat-bottom, chine, etc.):

20. Hull construction (lapstrake, smooth-planked, riveted steel, etc.):

21. Stem (material, construction method, fastenings, dimensions, finish, condition):

22. Keel (material, construction method, fastenings, dimensions, finish, condition):

23. Stern Assembly (material, construction method, fastenings, dimensions, finish, condition):

24. Transom (material, construction method, fastenings, dimensions, finish, condition):

25. Planking (material, thickness, method of construction, fastenings, planks per side, caulking material, finish, condition):

26. Frames, futtocks, and floor timbers (material, construction method, fastenings, dimensions, spacing, finish, condition):

27. Deck and deck beams (material, construction method, fastenings, dimensions, finish, condition):

28. Rudder, centerboard, daggerboard (material, construction method, fastenings, dimensions, finish, condition):

29. Gunwale, including breasthook, quarterknees, rub rails, rowlock pads and sockets, inwales and outwales (material, construction method, fastenings, dimensions, finish, condition):

SUPERSTRUCTURE

30. Deckhouses, trunk tops, hatches, etc. (material, construction method, fastenings, dimensions, finish, condition):

31. Holds, cabins, galleys, heads, lockers, etc. (number and type, area, furnishings, hold capacity):

PROPULSION

32. Engine and engine gear, including shaft, propeller, reduction gear, stuffing box, and fuel tanks (manufacturer, date of manufacture, model, horsepower, fuel type, reduction gear ratio, shaft material and diameter, propeller material, propeller diameter, number of propeller blades, fuel tank material, fuel tank capacity):

33. Sails (number and type, material, dimensions, condition):

34. Masts and spars (number and type, materials, construction method, dimensions, finish, condition):

35. Rigging, including chainplates (material, construction method, fastenings, dimensions, condition):

36. Oars (number and type, material, construction method, dimensions, condition):

COMMUNICATION AND NAVIGATION

37. Radio, radar, depth recorder, LORAN, radio direction finder (RDF), compass, automatic pilot, etc. (number and type, manufacturer, date of manufacture, model):

MACHINERY

38. Winches, power blocks, donkey engines, pot haulers, net rollers, etc. (manufacturer, date of manufacture, model, dimensions, condition):

FISHING GEAR

39. Nets, trawls, dredges, pots, traps, etc. (number and type, manufacturer, date of manufacture, dimensions, condition):

OTHER DETAILS

40.

41. Measured drawings executed by fieldworker(s)? ___YES ___NO. If YES, indicate number and type of drawings (lines plan, construction plan, outboard profile, section plan, deck plan, sail and rigging plans, mechanical propulsion plan, plans of details):

42. Photographs taken by fieldworkers? ___YES ___NO. If YES, attach completed PHOTOGRAPH INFORMATION FORMS.

43. Other available materials, including original plans, builder's half models, moulds, templates, photographs (number, type, location):

BIBLIOGRAPHY

44. Sources of information supplied above:

BUILDING DOCUMENTATION FORM*

Fieldworker: _____

Project: _____

Date: _____

1. Name of structure: _____

2. Location/address of structure: _____

3. Name and address of present owner: _____

_____

4. Name of present occupant/user: _____

5. Present use of structure: _____

6. Significance of structure (significance to community, architectural significance, connection to important

    people or events): _____

_____

_____

_____

7. Date of construction: _____

8. Names and addresses of architect, designer, builder, supplier: _____

_____

_____

_____

_____

*This form is adapted from instructions for the documentation of buildings contained in pages 97–118 of *Recording Historic Buildings* by Harley J. McKee.

9. Names of previous owners and dates of ownership:

_____

_____

_____

_____

10. Previous uses of structure (include dates):

_____

_____

_____

11. Description of original structure (basic dimensions, manner of construction, materials used, furnishings,
     equipment):

_____

_____

12. Description (with dates) of known alterations and additions:

_____

_____

_____

_____

ARCHITECTURAL DESCRIPTION

13. Summary (number of stories, overall dimensions, basic layout, architectural style):

_____

_____

_____

_____

14. Exterior description:

   a. foundations (height, thickness, materials, condition):

   b. walls (materials, color, texture, ornamental features, condition):

   c. structural system (wall type, floor systems, roof framing, joinery, details, condition):

   d. porches, stoops, terraces, bulkheads (location, kind, form, details, condition):

   e. chimneys (number, location, size, materials, condition):

   f. windows (fenestration, type, glazing, trim, shutters, condition):

   g. roofs (shape, covering, features, condition):

15. Interior description:

   a. floor plans:

   b. stairways (location, number, individual description, condition):

c. flooring (type, finish, condition):

d. doors and doorways (number, type, materials, color, finish, location, dimensions, condition):

e. trim (woodwork, cabinets, ornamental features, fireplace treatment):

f. hardware (hinges, knobs, locks, and latches):

g. mechanical and electrical equipment (heating, lighting, and plumbing systems and related fixtures, and machinery):

SITE AND SURROUNDINGS

16. Orientation and setting (compass directions, immediate environment, topography, approaches):

17. Landscape design:

18. Outbuildings (type, materials, features, condition):

OTHER DETAILS

19.

ILLUSTRATIVE MATERIALS

20. Measured drawings executed by fieldworker(s)? ___YES ___NO. If YES, indicate number and type of drawings (location plan, plot plan, floor plans, exterior elevations, general sections, decorative details, structural details):

21. Photographs taken by fieldworkers? ___YES ___NO. If YES, attach completed PHOTOGRAPH INFORMATION FORMS.

BIBLIOGRAPHY

22. Sources of information supplied above:

ARTIFACT LOAN FORM

I hereby give permission to the _____ Project to borrow the following artifact(s) belonging to me: _____

_____

I understand that the Project is borrowing my artifact(s) for the purpose of:

_____

_____
(owner signature)

_____
(date)

I, _____, acknowledge receipt of the artifact(s) listed above on behalf of the _____ Project. The Project agrees to return the loaned artifact(s) in the same condition it was received, on or before _____ (date).

_____
(Project representative)

_____
(date)

SAMPLE FIELDNOTES

Fieldworker: David Taylor
Project: Maritime Heritage Survey
Date: November 6, 1986
Place: Apalachicola, Florida

Nancy Nusz and I left our rented cottage at 6:45 a.m. to meet with Apalachicola oysterman Ken Folsom and spend the day with him aboard his oyster skiff. We had breakfast at a local diner, and arrived at Ken's boat house on Water Street at about 7:45 a.m. We waited around until Ken showed up at a little before 8:00.

Ken was born in 1955 and is originally from Ft. Walton Beach, Florida. He worked in radio broadcasting for several years and decided he preferred the slower pace of fishing. He has been oystering for six years.

We boarded his boat and headed west in the bay, arriving at the intended oystering spot, called "North Spur," within about twenty minutes. Along the way we passed by a leased oyster bed marked by pilings driven into the bay floor. Ken had marked out the area he wanted to oyster in previously by putting out buoys (one-gallon-size plastic jugs). For finding a more specific location, he used "the ranges." That is, he lined up landmarks, in this case a clump of trees above a small building on the shore. He records this information in a "range book"—a notebook that he keeps on board. Ken dropped anchor (an auto crank shaft) and began using his tongs to bring up oysters which he deposited on the "culling board"—a piece of plywood, with two-by-four rails, set athwartships.

Within a few minutes, another oysterman came by and dropped anchor a short distance away. Ken told us that he is Cletus Anderson, the oysterman from whom Ken learned.

After 20 minutes or so, Cletus, curious about Nancy and me, Ken speculated, came closer and introduced himself. He oystered close to us for the rest of the day and presented us with a good opportunity to speak to another oysterman, and gave us a chance to photograph activity on another boat. Cletus's boat was built by Sonny Polous of Apalachicola.

Ken cheerfully explained his tonging activities including: developing the ability to learn what's on the bottom by listening to the sound made by the tongs, and by feeling vibrations of the tongs with hands and feet; developing balance, and using leverage to reduce effort and strain when tonging; noticing change in shell color in relationship to shell location (e.g., on edge of bar).

Ken's tongs are 12 ft. long and made by Corky Richards of Apalachicola. Cletus's are 14 footers and also made by Corky. (Cletus's tongs have 18 teeth.) Ken also uses his tongs to change the position of his boat on the bed (i.e., he uses them like a pole).

Ken explained that some oystermen carry poles or a chain which they use to determine the location of oyster beds. Cletus uses a chain. Later in the day, we observed a man pass by who was using a pole in this manner while his boat was underway.

State regulations say that oysters must be at least three inches long. Ken has a notch in the rail of his culling board—slightly longer than three inches—which he uses as a gauge.

Oystering by Ken and Cletus continued throughout the day. Nancy and I took photos and recorded observations. Ken and Cletus seemed happy to answer our questions. When speaking about weatherlore, Cletus said of the local winds and their correlation to fishing success:

"East is the least;
 the West is the best."

Around 1:30 p.m., Nancy and I gave Ken a hand by culling the oysters which had accumulated on the culling board. Ken had culled a large batch by himself earlier. This not only helped us pass the time, but also helped us better understand how to cull, and how to recognize certain types of oysters. Local names for oysters included:

"burr"— a cluster of oysters

"coon"—oyster which grows close to shore—close enough for racoons to harvest them

"scissor"—long, narrow oyster

Another term—"hogging"—means to harvest while standing directly on the bed rather than in a boat. "Lick" means a pass over the bed with the tongs ("my last lick was a good one").

Ken prefers to sell "select" oysters. That is, single oysters that he has separated from others, if necessary, with his culling iron. He receives a higher price for selects than for oysters less thoroughly culled. He takes great pride in this, and remarked on the difficulty inherent in changing this preference in order to sell larger quantities of oysters of an inferior grade.

There was much discussion during the day by Ken and Cletus about the "freedom" of oystering, and being one's own boss. Ken hurried to finish his culling in order to leave the beds by 4 p.m. We then went to the Department of Natural Resources checkpoint by the Lighthouse Restaurant (on Rt. 98). After that we went up the river to Ken's buyer's place (Seasweet Seafood on Commerce Street, run by Roger Newton, mayor of Apalachicola). There, oysters are weighed, washed and graded as we watched. We returned to the dock at about 5:15 p.m.

Fieldworker Ormond Loomis taking the lines of twelve-foot fishing boat owned by Frank "Sonny Boy" Segree of Eastpoint, Florida. He is using an adjustable square to measure the distance between the baseline and the bottom of the boat at Station 2. Photo by David A. Taylor (FMP86–BDT038/8)

TAKING THE LINES OF A SMALL BOAT

The methods used to take the lines of a boat vary according to its size, shape, weight, and location. Take, for example, the case of a small fishing boat used by a fisherman in Eastpoint, Florida. The boat selected for documentation was built in 1981 by Frank "Sonny Boy" Segree for his own use floundering and gill netting in the waters of Apalachicola Bay. The twelve-foot craft is constructed entirely of cypress and is held together with galvanized fastenings. Segree calls the boat a "dinky," and because it is small, light, and quite simple in form, it is an easy craft to document.

The first step in taking the lines of the dinky is to lift it off the ground and place it, bottom-side up, on top of a pair of benches. This is done to make it easier to make the necessary measurements. The boat is then leveled with the use of a carpenter's level. Following this, a plumb bob is used to establish perpendicular lines. One line touches the center of the after-most part of the transom, and the other touches the center of the forward-most part of the stem. Thin stakes are driven securely into the ground to mark the forward perpendicular (FP), and the after perpendicular (AP). Next, a baseline is established by stretching a stout string between the stakes. The string is positioned so that it runs horizontally, directly above the centerline of the boat. Then, a carpenter's square and a line level are used to verify that a right angle has been formed at the point where the string is tied to the stakes. At this stage, the basic reference points for the first series of measurements have been established.

Next, various measuring devices, including a carpenter's square, a six-foot folding rule, and a sixteen-foot tape measure, are used for a series of measurements. All measurements are checked, and then immediately recorded in a notebook. The first measurement

Table of Offsets for twelve-foot "dinky" by Frank "Sonny Boy" Segree, Eastpoint, Florida. Lines taken off at Eastpoint, Florida, by Ormond Loomis and David Taylor, November 14, 1986. (Measurements given in feet, inches, and eighths.)

		Stem	Station 1	Station 2	Station 3	Transom
1.	Sheer	1–7–6	1–4–0	1–2–6	1–3–1	1–4–4
	Bottom	0–6–0	0–3–3	0–1–6	0–2–2	0–4–4
2.	Sheer	0–0–4	1–6–0	1–11–4	1–11–4	1–9–3
	Bottom	0–0–4	1–2–7	1–9–5	1–9–2	1–7–2
	Skeg	0–0–0	0–0–0	0–0–0	0–0–6	0–0–6

(1) height from base line. (2) half breadths from center line.

Table of offsets for twelve-foot fishing boat.

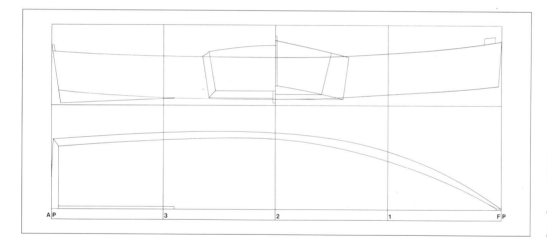

AP   3   2   1   FP

Lines plan of twelve-foot boat, including profile (top), body plan (top-center), and half-breadth (bottom). Drawing by David A. Taylor

is of the overall length of the boat. Then, the maximum breadth of the bottom of the boat is measured. This point of maximum breadth is designated as Station 2. Two other stations, Station 1 and Station 3, are then established at points halfway between Station 2 and the FP, and halfway between Station 2 and the AP, respectively. The breadths of the bottom at Stations 1 and 3, and the transom are then measured. Full breadths at each of the three stations and the transom are divided in half and recorded in the table of offsets under "half breadths."

The next measurements correspond to the distance between the center line of the boat and the string, or baseline, at all three stations, the bottom of the stem, and the bottom of the transom. These measurements are taken off and recorded in the table of offsets under "heights above base."

Following these measurements, the "profile" (that is, the view from the side) of the stem and stern are recorded. These measurements illustrate the shapes of the stem and stern with reference to FP and baseline, and AP and baseline, respectively. Since the stem and stern of this craft are both straight, these measurements are taken off very easily.

The next measurements record the "sheer heights," the distances between the baseline and the top edge of the hull at each station. Taking these measurements requires some degree of concentration, since it is necessary to ensure that imaginary horizontal lines running outboard from the base above the stations are perpendicular to vertical lines at the sheer. These measurements are recorded in the table of offsets under "sheer heights."

The next measurements are the dimensions of other features of the boat: the outboard face of the transom, the skeg, and the rub rail. The thickness of the planking is measured as well.

At this point, all critical outboard measurements have been taken, and the boat is turned over so that interior measurements can be recorded. Important interior features to measure include: the stem head, including cross-section, and height above the sheer; thwarts; thwart risers; keelson; and chine battens. Finally, photographs, both black and white and color, are taken of the craft from a variety of angles. Close-up shots are taken of important or unique construction details. Later, using all measurements collected, a lines drawing of the dinky is produced. This drawing graphically represents the essential contours of the hull.

Bibliography

ARCHITECTURE

Blumenson, John. *Identifying American Architecture: A Pictorial Guide to Styles and Terms, 1600–1945.* 2d rev. ed. New York: W.W. Norton, 1981.

Glassie, Henry. *Folk Housing in Middle Virginia: A Structural Analysis of Historic Artifacts.* Knoxville: University of Tennessee Press, 1975.

Howe, Barbara J., Dolores A. Fleming, Emory L. Kemp, and Ruth Ann Overbeck. *Houses and Homes: Exploring Their History.* Nashville: American Association for State and Local History, 1987.

McAlester, Virginia, and Lee McAlester. *A Field Guide to American Houses.* New York: Alfred A. Knopf, 1984.

McKee, Harley J. *Recording Historic Buildings: The Historic American Buildings Survey.* Washington: U.S. Department of the Interior, National Park Service, 1970.

Peatross, C. Ford, ed. *Historic America: Buildings, Structures, and* Sites. Washington: Library of Congress, 1983.

Renk, Thomas B. "A Guide to Recording Structural Details of Historic Buildings." *Historical Archaeology* 3 (1969): 34–48.

BIBLIOGRAPHIES AND DIRECTORIES

Acheson, James M. "Anthropology of Fishing." *Annual Review of Anthropology* 10 (1981), 275–316.

Albion, Robert Greenhalgh. *Naval and Maritime History: An Annotated Bibliography.* Mystic, Ct.: The Marine Historical Association, Inc., 1972.

Bartis, Peter, and Mary Hufford, comps. *Maritime Folklife Resources: A Directory and Index.* Publications of the American Folklife Center, no. 5. Washington: Library of Congress, 1980.

Landberg, Leif, comp. *A Bibliography for the Anthropological Study of Fishing Industries and Maritime Communities* and *Supplement, 1973–1977.* Kingston, R.I.: University of Rhode Island, International Center for Marine Resources Development, 1973 and 1979, respectively.

Marshall, Howard W. *American Folk Architecture: A Selected Bibliography.* Publications of the American Folklife Center, no. 8. Washington: Library of Congress, 1981.

National Trust for Historic Preservation. *Directory of Maritime Heritage Resources.* Washington: National Trust for Historic Preservation, 1984.

BOATS AND BOATBUILDING

Anderson, Richard K. *Guidelines for Recording Historic Ships.* Washington: National Park Service, U.S. Department of the Interior, Historic American Engineering Record, 1988.

Blessing of the shrimp fleet in the spring at Petit Caillou Bayou, Chauvin, Louisiana. Photo courtesy of the Louisiana Department of Tourism

Brewington, Marion V. *Chesapeake Bay Log Canoes and Bugeyes.* Cambridge, Md.: Cornell Maritime Press, 1963.

Chapelle, Howard I. *American Small Sailing Craft: Their Design Development and Construction.* New York: W.W. Norton, 1951.

———. *Boatbuilding: A Complete Handbook of Wooden Boat Construction.* New York: W.W. Norton, 1941.

———. *The National Watercraft Collection.* 2d ed. Washington: Smithsonian Institution Press; Camden, Me.: International Marine Publishing Co., 1976.

Comeaux, Malcolm L. "Origin and Evolution of Mississippi River Fishing Craft." *Pioneer America* 10 (1978): 73–97.

Day, Arno. *The Lines Plan.* 3 Pts. Sea-TV: New Haven, Ct., 1990. Two thirty-minute videotapes, and one sixty-minute videotape.

Delgado, James P., comp. *Preliminary Inventory of Historic Large Vessels Preserved in the United States.* Washington: U.S. Department of the Interior, National Park Service, The National Maritime Initiative, 1987.

———. *Preliminary Inventory of Historic Small Craft Collections.* Washington: U.S. Department of the Interior, National Park Service, The National Maritime Initiative, 1987.

Gardner, John. "Taking Lines Off Bigger Boats." *National Fisherman* 67, no.1 (May 1986): 58.

———. "Taking Off Lines Allows Duplication of Existing Boats." *National Fisherman* 66, no. 12 (April 1986): 44–45.

———. *The Dory Book.* Camden, Me.: International Marine Publishing Co., 1978.

———. "Triangulation Method is Well Suited to Lifting Lines." *National Fisherman* 67, no. 4 (August 1986): 65–67.

Gillmer, Thomas C. *Working Watercraft: A Survey of Surviving Local Boats of America and Europe.* Camden, Me.: International Marine Publishing Co., 1978.

Greenhill, Basil. *Archaeology of the Boat: A New Introductory Study.* Middletown, Ct.: Wesleyan University Press, 1976.

Guthorn, Peter J. *The Seabright Skiff and Other Jersey Shore Boats.* Brunswick, N.J.: Rutgers University Press, 1971.

Holmes, Tommy. *The Hawaiian Canoe.* Kauai, Hi.: Editions Limited, 1981.

Hornell, James. *Water Transport: Origin and Early Development.* Cambridge: Cambridge University Press, 1946.

Johnson, Paula J., and David A. Taylor. "Beyond the Boat: Documenting the Cultural Context." In *Boats: A Field Manual for the Documentation of Small Craft,* ed. Paul Lipke. Nashville: American Association for State and Local History, forthcoming.

Knipmeyer, William P. "Folk Boats of Eastern French Louisiana." Edited by Henry Glassie. In *American Folklife,* ed. Don Yoder, 105–49. Austin and London: University of Texas Press, 1976.

Lipke, Paul, ed. *Boats: A Field Manual for the Documentation of Small Craft.* Nashville: American Association for State and Local History, forthcoming.

———. *Plank on Frame: The Who, What and Where of 150 Boatbuilders.* Camden, Me.: International Marine Publishing Co.,1981.

Lunt, C. Richard K. "Lobsterboat Building on the Eastern Coast of Maine: A Comparative Study." Ph.D. diss., Indiana University, 1976.

———. "The St. Lawrence Skiff and the Folklore of Boats." *New York Folklore Quarterly* 29 (1973): 154–268.

Bibliography

McKee, Eric. *Clenched Lap or Clinker: An Appreciation of Boatbuilding Technique.* London: National Maritime Museum, 1972.

———. *Working Boats of Britain: Their Shape and Purpose.* Greenwich: Conway Maritime Press,1983.

Moonsammy, Rita. "Smart Boats, Able Captains: The Schooner as Metaphor." *New Jersey Folklife* 12 (1987): 38–44.

Phillips-Birt, Douglas. *The Naval Architecture of Small Craft.* London: Hutchinson and Co., 1957.

Salaman, R. A. "Tools of the Shipwright, 1650–1925." *Folk-Life* 5 (1967): 19–51.

Shock, Edison Irwin. "How I Took Pinkletink's Lines." In *The Catboat Book*, ed. John M. Leavens, 38–41. Camden, Me.: International Marine Publishing Co. for the Catboat Association, 1973.

Simmons, Walter J. *Lapstrake Boatbuilding.* Camden, Me.: International Marine Publishing Co., 1978.

———. *Lapstrake Boatbuilding Volume 2.* Camden, Me.: International Marine Publishing Co., 1980.

———. *Lines, Lofting and Half Models.* Lincolnville, Me.: Ducktrap Woodworking, 1991.

Taylor, David A. *Boat Building in Winterton, Trinity Bay, Newfoundland.* Canadian Centre for Folk Culture Studies, Paper no. 41. Ottawa: National Museum of Man, 1982.

———. "Taking the Lines." *Woodenboat* 19 (Nov.-Dec. 1977): 42–45.

Time-Life Books. *The Classic Boat.* Alexandria, Va.: Time-Life Books, 1977.

Vaitses, Allan H. *Lofting.* Camden, Me.: International Marine Publishing Co., 1980.

CULTURAL CONSERVATION AND HISTORIC PRESERVATION

Delgado, James P. "Grim Realities, High Hopes, Moderate Gains: The State of Historic Ship Preservation." *Cultural Resources Management Bulletin* 12, no. 4 (1989): 1, 3–4.

Delgado, James P., and a National Park Service Maritime Task Force. *Nominating Historic Vessels and Shipwrecks to the National Register of Historic Places.* National Register Bulletin 20. Washington: U.S. Department of the Interior, National Park Service, Interagency Resources Division, n.d.

Derry, Anne, H. Ward Jandl, Carol D. Shull, and Jan Thorman. *Guidelines for Local Surveys: A Guide for Preservation Planning.* National Register Bulletin 24. Rev. ed. Washington: National Register of Historic Places, Interagency Resources Division, U.S. Department of the Interior, 1985.

Hufford, Mary. *One Space, Many Places: Folklife and Land Use in New Jersey's Pinelands National Reserve.* Publications of the American Folklife Center, no. 15. Washington: Library of Congress, 1986.

King, Thomas F., Patricia Parker, and Gary Berg. *Anthropology in Historic Preservation: Caring for Culture's Clutter.* New York: Academic Press, 1977.

Loomis, Ormond, coord. *Cultural Conservation: The Protection of Cultural Heritage in the United States.* Publications of the American Folklife Center, no. 10. Washington: Library of Congress, 1983.

ETHICS

American Anthropological Association. *Professional Ethics: Statements and Procedures of the American Anthropological Association.* Washington: American Anthropological Association, 1983.

EXHIBITS

Witteborg, Lothar P. *Good Show: A Practical Guide for Temporary Exhibitions.* Washington: Smithsonian Institution Traveling Exhibition Service, 1981.

FIELDWORK GUIDES

Allen, Barbara, and Lynwood Montell. *From Memory to History: Using Oral Sources in Local Historical Research.* Nashville: American Association for State and Local History, 1981.

Bartis, Peter. *Folklife & Fieldwork: A Layman's Introduction to Field Techniques.* Rev. and expanded ed. Publications of the American Folklife Center, no. 3. Washington: Library of Congress, 1990.

Baum, Willa K. *Oral History and the Local Historical Society.* 3rd rev. ed. Nashville: American Association for State and Local History, 1987.

Burgess, Robert G. *Field Research: A Sourcebook and Field Manual.* Contemporary Social Research Series: 4. London: George Allen and Unwin, 1982.

Danzer, Gerald A. *Public Places: Exploring Their History.* Nashville: American Association for State and Local History, 1987.

Georges, Robert A., and Michael Owen Jones. *People Studying People: The Human Element in Fieldwork.* Berkeley and Los Angeles: University of California Press, 1980.

Goldstein, Kenneth S. *A Guide for Field Workers in Folklore.* Hatboro, Pa.: Folklore Associates, 1964.

Gorden, Raymond L. *Interviewing: Strategy, Techniques and Tactics.* Homewood, Ill.: The Dorsey Press, 1969.

Ives, Edward D. *The Tape-Recorded Interview: A Manual for Field Workers in Folklore and Oral History.* Knoxville: University of Tennessee Press, 1980.

Jackson, Bruce. *Fieldwork.* Urbana and Chicago: University of Illinois Press, 1987.

Kammen, Carol. *On Doing Local History: Reflections on What Local Historians Do, Why, and What it Means.* Nashville: American Association for State and Local History, 1986.

Kyvig, David E., and Myron A. Marty. *Nearby History: Exploring the Past Around You.* Nashville: American Association for State and Local History, 1982.

Northeast Archives of Folklore and Oral History. *An Oral Historian's Work, with Dr. Edward Ives.* Orono, Me.: Northeast Archives of Folklore and Oral History, 1987. Thirty-min. videotape.

Roberts, Warren E. "Fieldwork: Recording Material Culture." In *Folklore and Folklife: An Introduction,* ed. Richard M. Dorson, 431–44. Chicago: University of Chicago Press, 1972.

Spradley, James P. *Participant Observation.* New York: Holt, Rinehart and Winston, 1980.

————. *The Ethnographic Interview.* New York: Holt, Rinehart and Winston, 1979.

Spradley, James P., and David W. McCurdy, *The Cultural Experience: Ethnography in Complex Society.* Chicago: Science Research Association, 1972.

Thompson, Paul. *The Voice of the Past: Oral History.* Oxford: Oxford University Press, 1978.

FOLKLIFE STUDIES, INTRODUCTIONS

Brown, Linda Keller, and Kay Mussell, eds. *Ethnic and Regional Foodways in the United States: The Performance of Group Identity.* Knoxville: University of Tennessee Press, 1984.

Bibliography

Brunvand, Jan H. *The Study of American Folklore: An Introduction.* New York: W.W. Norton, 1968.

Byington, Robert H., ed. *Working Americans: Contemporary Approaches to Occupational Folklife.* Smithsonian Folklife Studies, no. 3. Los Angeles: California Folklore Society, 1978.

Dorson, Richard. *Buying the Wind.* Chicago: University of Chicago Press, 1964.

Dorson, Richard M., ed. *Folklore and Folklife: An Introduction.* Chicago: University of Chicago Press, 1972.

————. *Handbook of American Folklore.* Bloomington: Indiana University Press, 1986

Glassie, Henry. *Pattern in the Material Folk Culture of the Eastern United States.* Philadelphia: University of Pennsylvania Press, 1968.

Oring, Elliott, ed. *Folk Groups and Folklore Genres: An Introduction.* Logan, Ut.: Utah State University Press, 1986.

Toelken, Barre. *The Dynamics of Folklore.* Boston: Houghton Mifflin Co., 1979.

Yoder, Don, ed. *American Folklife.* Austin: University of Texas Press, 1976.

Zeitlin, Steven J., Amy J. Kotkin, and Holly Cutting Baker. *A Celebration of American Family Folklore: Tales and Traditions from the Smithsonian Collection.* New York: Pantheon, 1982.

FOLKLIFE STUDIES, MARITIME

Abrahams, Roger D., Kenneth S. Goldstein, and Wayland D. Hand, eds., with the assistance of Maggie Craig. *By Land and By Sea: Studies in the Folklore of Work and Leisure Honoring Horace P. Beck on his Sixty-Fifth Birthday.* Hatboro, Pa.: Legacy Books, 1985.

Acheson, James M. "Territories of the Maine Lobstermen." *Natural History* 81 (1972): 60–69.

————. *The Lobster Gangs of Maine.* Hanover, N.H.: University Press of New England, 1988.

Andersen, Raoul, ed. *North Atlantic Maritime Cultures: Anthropological Essays on Changing Adaptations.* The Hague: Mouton Publishers, 1979.

————. "Those Fishermen Lies: Custom and Competition in North Atlantic Fisherman Communication." *Ethnos* 38 (1973): 153–64.

Andersen, Raoul, and Cato Wadel, eds. *North Atlantic Fishermen: Anthropological Essays on Modern Fishing.* Newfoundland Social and Economic Papers, no. 5. St. John's: Memorial University of Newfoundland, Institute of Social and Economic Research, 1972.

Anson, Peter F. *British Sea Fishermen.* London: William Collins, 1944.

————. *Fisher Folk-lore: Old Taboos and Superstitions among the Fisher Folk.* London: Faith Press, 1965.

————. *Fishermen and Fishing Ways.* London: George Harrup and Co., Ltd., 1932.

————. *Fishing Boats and Fisher Folk on the East Coast of Scotland.* London: J. M. Dent and Sons Ltd., 1930.

————. *Scots Fisherfolk.* Banff: Banffshire Journal Ltd., 1950.

Beck, Horace P. *Folklore and the Sea.* Mystic Seaport Marine Historical Association American Maritime Library, vol. 6. Middletown, Ct.: Wesleyan University Press, 1973.

Beck, Jane C. *The Legacy of the Lake: A Study Guide to the Folklife of the Lake Champlain Region.* Montpelier, Vt.: The Vermont Folklife Center, 1985.

Brandt, Andres von. *Fish Catching Methods of the World*. 3rd rev. and enlarged ed. Farnham, England: Fishing News Books Ltd., 1984.

Browning, Robert J. *Fisheries of the North Pacific: History, Species, Gear & Processes*. Rev. ed. Anchorage, Ak.: Alaska Northwest Publishing Co., 1980.

Butler, Gary R. "Culture, Cognition, and Communication: Fishermen's Location Finding in L'Anse-a-Canards, Newfoundland." *Canadian Folklore Canadien* 5, nos. 1–2 (1983): 7–21.

Calander, Harriet Bell. *History of Fish and Fishing in the Upper Mississippi River*. Davenport, Ia.: Upper Mississippi River Conservation Commission, 1954.

Carey, George. *A Faraway Time and Place: Lore of the Eastern Shore*. Washington and New York: Robert B. Luce, Inc., 1971.

Comeaux, Malcolm L. *Atchafalaya Swamp Life: Settlement and Folk Occupations*. Baton Rouge: Louisiana State University Press, 1972.

Curry, Jane. *The River's in My Blood: Riverboat Pilots Tell Their Stories*. Lincoln and London: University of Nebraska Press, 1983.

Eunson, Jerry. "The Fair-Isle Fishing-Marks." *Scottish Studies* 5 (1961): 181–98.

Feinberg, Richard. *Polynesian Seafaring and Navigation: Ocean Travel in Anutan Culture and Society*. Kent, Ohio, and London: The Kent State University Press, 1988.

Florida Department of State. *Fishing All My Days*. White Springs, Fl.: Florida Department of State, Bureau of Florida Folklife Programs, 1986. Videotape.

Forman, Shepard. "Cognition and the Catch: The Location of Fishing Spots in a Brazilian Coastal Village. *Ethnology* 6, no. 4 (1967): 417–26.

Fricke, Peter H., ed. *Seafarer & Community: Towards a Social Understanding of Seafaring*. London: Croom Helm, 1973.

Frye, John. *The Men All Singing: The Story of Menhaden Fishing*. Norfolk, Va.: Dunning, 1978.

Gersuny, Carl, and John J. Poggie, Jr. "Danger and Fishermen's Taboos." *Maritimes* 16, no. 1 (1972): 3–4.

Gilmore, Janet C. *The World of the Oregon Fishboat: A Study in Maritime Folklife*. Ann Arbor, Mi.: UMI Research Press, 1986.

Gladwin, Thomas. *East is a Big Bird: Navigation and Logic on Puluwat Atoll*. Cambridge: Harvard University Press, 1970.

Goode, George Brown, ed. *The Fisheries and Fishery Industries of the United States*. 7 vols. Washington: Government Printing Office, 1884–87.

Green, Ben. *Finest Kind: A Celebration of a Florida Fishing Village*. Macon, Ga.: Mercer University Press, 1985.

Griffin, Carl, III, and Alaric Faulkner, and including the reminiscences of Alberta Poole Rowe. *Coming of Age on Damariscove Island, Maine*. *Northeast Folklore* 21 (1980).

Gunda, Bela, ed. *The Fishing Culture of the World: Studies in Ethnology, Cultural Ecology and Folklore*. 2 vols. Budapest: Akademiai Kiado, 1984.

Hall, C. Eleanor. "Ice Fishing on Lake Champlain." *New York Folklore Quarterly* 21, no. 1 (1965): 19–25.

Hasslöf, Olof. "Sources of Maritime History and Methods of Research." *Mariner's Mirror* 52 (1966): 127–44.

Hasslöf, Olof, Henning Henningsen, and Arne Emil Christensen, Jr., eds. *Ships and Shipyards, Sailors and Fishermen: Introduction to Maritime Ethnology*. Copenhagen: Rosenkilde and Bagger, 1972.

Bibliography

Henningsen, H. "Taboo Words Among Seamen and Fishermen." *Mariners' Mirror* 43 (1957): 336–37.

Hornell, James. *Fishing in Many Waters.* Cambridge: The University Press, 1950.

Huntington, Gale, ed. *Tom Tilton: Coaster and Fisherman. Northeast Folklore* 23 (1982).

Jenkins, J. Geraint. *Nets and Coracles.* Newton Abbot, England, and North Pomfret, Vt.: David & Charles, 1974.

Johnson, Paula J., ed. *Working the Water: The Commercial Fisheries of Maryland's Patuxent River.* Charlottesville, Va.: University Press of Virginia, 1988.

Kennedy, Don H. *Ship Names: Origins and Usages During 45 Centuries.* Charlottesville, Va.: University Press of Virginia for The Mariners Museum, 1974.

Kochiss, John M. *Oystering from New York to Boston.* Middletown, Ct.: Wesleyan University Press for Mystic Seaport, 1974.

Kozma, LuAnne Gaykowski, ed. *Living at a Lighthouse: Oral Histories from the Great Lakes.* Allen Park, Mi.: Great Lakes Lighthouse Keepers Association, 1987.

Lewis, David. *We, the Navigators.* Honolulu: The University Press of Hawaii, 1972.

Lloyd, Timothy C., and Patrick B. Mullen. *Lake Erie Fishermen: Work, Tradition, and Identity.* Urbana and Chicago: University of Illinois Press, 1990.

Lund, Jens. "Danger and Delight: Environmental-Experience Narratives in Southern New Jersey." *New Jersey Folklife* 12 (1987): 26–31.

———. "Fishing as a Folk Occupation in the Lower Ohio Valley." Ph.D. diss., Indiana University, 1982.

Maril, Robert Lee. *Texas Shrimpers: Community, Capitalism, and the Sea.* College Station: Texas A & M University Press, 1983.

Martin, Kenneth R., and Nathan R. Lipfert. *Lobstering and the Maine Coast.* Bath, Me.: Maine Maritime Museum, 1985.

Matthiessen, Peter. *Men's Lives: The Surfmen and Baymen of the South Fork.* New York: Random House, 1986.

Miller, Jennifer, ed. *Coastal Affair.* Special issue of *Southern Exposure* 10, no. 3 (May/June 1982).

Moonsammy, Rita. "Smart Boats, Able Captains: The Schooner as Metaphor." *New Jersey Folklife* 12 (1987): 38–44

Moonsammy, Rita Zorn, David Steven Cohen, and Lorraine E. Williams, eds. *Pinelands Folklife.* New Brunswick, N.J., and London: Rutgers University Press, 1987.

Mullen, Patrick B. *I Heard the Old Fishermen Say: Folklore of the Texas Gulf Coast.* Austin: University of Texas Press, 1978.

Orbach, Michael K. *Hunters, Seamen and Entrepreneurs: The Tuna Fishermen of San Diego.* Berkeley: University of California Press, 1977.

Pearson, John C., ed. *The Fish and Fisheries of Colonial North America: A Documentary History of the Fishery Resources of the United States and Canada.* 9 vols. Rockville, Md.: National Marine Fisheries Service, 1972.

Pilcher, William W. *The Portland Longshoremen: A Dispersed Community.* New York: Holt, Rinehart, and Winston, 1972.

Poggie, John J., Jr., and Carl Gersuny. *Fishermen of Galilee: The Human Ecology of a New England Coastal Community.* University of Rhode Island Marine Bulletin Series, no. 17. Kingston, R.I.: University of Rhode Island, 1974.

———. "Risk and Ritual: An Interpretation of Fishermen's Folklore in a New England Community." *Journal of American Folklore* 85 (1972): 66–72.

Posen, I. Sheldon. *You Hear the Ice Talking: The Ways of People and Ice on Lake Champlain.* Published in conjunction with the Lake Champlain Ice Exhibition, Clinton County Historical Museum, Plattsburgh, N.Y., January-April 1987. Plattsburgh, N.Y.: The Clinton-Essex-Franklin Library System, 1986.

Sainsbury, John C. *Commercial Fishing Methods: An Introduction to Vessels and Gear.* London: Fishing News (Books) Ltd., 1971.

Smith, M. Estelle, ed. *Those Who Live From the Sea: A Study in Maritime Anthropology.* St. Paul, Mn.: West Publishing Co., 1977.

Stiles, R. Geoffrey. "Fishermen, Wives and Radios: Aspects of Communications in a Newfoundland Fishing Community." In *North Atlantic Fishermen: Anthropological Essays on Modern Fishing*, eds. Raoul Andersen and Cato Wadel, 35–60. Newfoundland Social and Economic Papers, no. 5. St. John's: Memorial University of Newfoundland, Institute of Social and Economic Research, 1972.

Taylor, David A. "Songs About Fishing: Examples of Contemporary Maritime Songs." *Canadian Folklore Canadien* 12, no. 2 (1990): 85–99.

Taylor, Lawrence J. *Dutchmen on the Bay: The Ethnohistory of a Contractual Community.* Philadelphia: University Of Pennsylvania Press, 1983.

Thompson, Paul, with Tony Wailey and Trevor Lummis. *Living the Fishing.* London: Routledge & Kegan Paul, 1983.

Tunstall, Jeremy. *The Fishermen.* London: MacGibbon and Kee, 1969.

Wood, Pamela, ed. *The Salt Book: Lobstering, Sea Moss Pudding, Stone Walls, Rum Running, Maple Syrup, Snowshoes, and Other Yankee Doings.* Garden City, N.Y.: Anchor Press/Doubleday, 1977.

———, ed. *Salt 2: Boatbuilding, Sailmaking, Island People, River Driving, Bean Hole Beans, Wooden Paddles, and More Yankee Doings.* Garden City, N.Y.: Anchor Press/Doubleday, 1980

FUND-RAISING

Bauer, David G. *The "How To" Grants Manual: Successful Grantseeking Techniques for Obtaining Public and Private Grants.* New York: American Council on Education, Macmillan, 1988.

Grasty, William K. *Successful Fundraising.* New York: Scribner, 1982.

Flanagan, Joan. *The Grass Roots Fundraising Book.* Chicago: Contemporary Books, 1982.

The Foundation Center. *The Foundation Directory.* 13th ed. New York: The Foundation Center, 1991.

LANDSCAPE

Lewis, Pierce. "Learning from Looking: Geographic and Other Writing about the American Cultural Landscape." *American Quarterly* 35, no. 3 (1983): 242–61.

Meinig, D.W., ed. *The Interpretation of Ordinary Landscapes: Geographical Essays.* Oxford: Oxford University Press, 1979

Pocius, Gerald L. *A Place to Belong: Community Order and Everyday Space in Calvert, Newfoundland.* Athens, Ga.: University of Georgia Press, 1991.

Tuan, Yi-Fu. *Space and Place: The Perspective of Experience.* Minneapolis: University of Minnesota Press, 1977.

———. *Topophilia: A Study of Environmental Perception, Attitudes, and Values.* Englewood Cliffs, N.J.: Prentice-Hall, 1974.

Bibliography

PHOTOGRAPHY

Brown, Bruce C. *Watershots: How to Take Better Photos On and Around the Water.* Camden, Me.: International Marine Publishing Co., 1988.

Collier, John, Jr., and Malcolm Collier. *Visual Anthropology: Photography as a Research Method.* Rev. and expanded ed. Albuquerque: University of New Mexico Press, 1986.

Dean, Jeff. *Architectural Photography: Techniques for Architects, Preservationists, Historians, Photographers, and Urban Planners.* Nashville: American Association for State and Local History, 1982.

Fleischhauer, Carl. "Sound Recording and Still Photography in the Field." In *Handbook of American Folklore,* ed. Richard M. Dorson, 384–90. Bloomington: Indiana University Press,1986.

Hedecoe, John. *The Photographer's Handbook.* Westminster, Md.: Alfred A. Knopf, Inc., 1977.

Horenstein, Henry. *Black and White Photography.* Boston: Little, Brown, 1983.

Jolly, Brad. *Videotaping Local History.* Nashville: American Association for State and Local History, 1982.

SOUND RECORDING

Burstein, Herman. *Questions and Answers About Tape Recording.* Blue Ridge Summitt, Pa.: TAB Books, 1974.

Clifford, Martin. *Microphones—How They Work & How to Use Them.* Blue Ridge Summit, Pa.: TAB Books, 1977.

Fleischhauer, Carl. "Sound Recording and Still Photography in the Field." In *Handbook of American Folklore,* ed. Richard M. Dorson, 384–90. Bloomington: Indiana University Press, 1986.

Westcott, Charles G., and Richard F. Dubbe. *Tape Recorders: How They Work.* New York: Bobbs Merrill, 1974.

TERMINOLOGY

Kerchove, René de. *International Maritime Dictionary: An Encyclopedic Dictionary of Useful Maritime Terms and Phrases, Together with Equivalents in French and German.* 2d rev. ed. New York: Van Nostrand Reinhold, 1983.